AGENDA AND IDEOLOGIES

THOUGHTS ON CONGRESS, COMMUNISM, FASCISM AND OTHERS

AGENDA AND IDEOLOGIES

THOUGHTS ON CONGRESS, COMMUNISM, FASCISM AND OTHERS

PRAFULL GORADIA

Vitasta

To Nayana, my wife, who was an article writer much before me and in many ways, has been the inspiration for what is contained in this volume

Published by
Vitasta Publishing Pvt Ltd
2/15, Ansari Road, Daryaganj
New Delhi-110 002
info@vitastapublishing.com

ISBN 978-81-949640-0-1

First Edition 2021
MRP ₹495

Edited by Veena Batra
Cover and layout by Somesh Kumar Mishra
Printed by Vikas Computer and Printers, New Delhi

Contents

Why This Book?

I can still remember, as a boy of ten in Calcutta, Independence accompanied by Partition on 15 August 1947. Over the last seven decades or more, one has witnessed change and more change. In some of the years it appears as if changes took place faster than the clock.

In 1958 I was given a telephone by my employers which had no dial. Today we have the latest and the best mobiles which do practically everything to facilitate life especially for the elderly. The Internet is another wondrous world, what to talk of the computer. There was not even a calculator in 1947. In that year, owning a radio set was a matter of status, be it a Murphy, a Philips or a Westinghouse. Next to appear was the black and white television, then came the colour TV and now we have a TV that can become a cinema at home.

In 1955, India became a socialist state, which might have had its uses at the time but it succeeded in stunting India's economic growth. We had to wait till 1991 to be so fiscally poor that we had to pledge our gold to London banks. This enabled Prime Minster Narasimha Rao to push socialism to the Bay of Bengal and inaugurate liberalism.

For nearly a millennium, Indians had learnt to suffer literally everything. This tide of humiliation turned with Ayodhya in 1992. It is taking time for people to realise that it was at Ayodhya that the wheel of history turned so decisively. In an uncanny way, it has given India its first ruler who rules for the people and the country and not for himself.

To recount the history of independent India would be a fascinating challenge, although this volume only expresses the wish. It is an album that reflects some areas of life in India and elsewhere during the last three or four decades.

POLITICS

To Bring Calm to the Northeast

READING *THE STATESMAN* of recent days as well as other journals, it appears that some of the writers have overlooked the origins of the problems which the Citizenship (Amendment) Bill is intended to solve. The people of Assam and the rest of the Northeast are worried about their cultures being overwhelmed by more immigrants coming in from Bangladesh as refugees. The fear is greater from the eastern areas like Mymensingh and Sylhet. People from the more western areas would go to West Bengal. The fear is legitimate but there is a remedy to relieve it.

Before offering the remedy, two points need to be made. One, the Assamese, whether Adivasis or the more modernised ones are dead scared of being outnumbered by the Bengali-speaking people whether Hindu or Muslim. Merely assuring the people that protecting their culture is as much the Centre's concern as securing the culture of the entire country, is not enough.

Unless one has lived or frequently travelled in Assam, it is difficult to appreciate what nightmares the Assamese experience when they think of infiltration. They are a gentle people with a soft, peace-loving nature. They have their own festivals. They were gifted by nature with plenty of land and even more, the rivers and water. They do not have to work too hard for survival. The climate is mostly warm and humid, and so is not congenial for hard work. They are not competitive by nature and understandably shudder at the fear of this ethos being disturbed by outsiders.

Believe it not, until two decades ago, it was a popular impression that the Congress strategy for winning elections in Assam was "Ali, Coolie and Bengali". Coolie implied the tea garden workers and their families. Ali and Bengali are self-explanatory; they are mostly people who had over the years immigrated into Assam. Even the tea garden workers were Adivasis brought from Jharkhand and neighbouring areas to plant and pluck the bushes. To this day, it is difficult to find an original Assamese who is a plucker in a tea garden. Therefore, the Congress depended on settlers from outside to win a majority vote.

When World War II broke out in Europe, the British declared that India too was a participant. The Congress expressed its grave disapproval at the government doing so without consulting the Indian leaders. In protest, all Congress provincial ministries resigned as did the one in Assam. The replacement was a Muslim League ministry led by Muhammed Saadulah. He concocted a new theory that the Adivasis in Assam were animists and not Hindus. The resulting arithmetic made the Muslims a near majority.

In 1947, MA Jinnah nearly convinced the British rulers

that Assam was a Muslim majority province and should go to Pakistan. Sheikh Mujibur Rahman, in his book *Eastern Pakistan*, stated that the tribals were not only not Hindus but also unfit for civilized life. The generally vague conclusion of the sympathisers for Pakistan was that East Bengal and Assam should be combined into one province, as was the case under the first partition of Bengal by Viceroy Lord Curzon in 1905. Fortunately, it was undone by 1911. Lord Pethick Lawrence, Secretary of State for India, also swallowed this theory about an amalgamation of the two.

The deception was almost done when Gopinath Bardoloi, the Assam Congress leader, rushed out to persuade those in power and with influence that the Jinnah contention was untrue. As a result, Assam was saved for India except for Sylhet district, which had a Muslim majority. Any wonder that the Assamese are afraid of allowing illegal migrants to settle? Incidentally, until 1874, Assam was a part of the Bengal Presidency. It was then separated and placed under the rule of a chief commissioner. To make Assam a viable separate province, three Bengali-speaking districts of the Presidency, namely, Goalpara, Sylhet and Cachar were merged into the new province. That is how Assam began to host Bengalis as well as Muslims. The going of Sylhet to East Pakistan in 1947 relieved this pressure to an extent.

Nevertheless, the partition added Bengalis to the population as Sylhet had been a sister district of Cachar and its people were at least 46 per cent Hindu. Moreover, Mymensingh district was also nearby to enable refugees to cross over. Due to the poverty of the landless peasants, Muslim infiltration also continued. West Pakistan monopolised the country's power and the eastern wing was treated as a colony. Emigration was perhaps the only way many an easterner could survive. The poorest came to Assam as well as West Bengal; the more resourceful went overseas. Called Bangladeshis since 1971, they have the reputation of being the world's number one migrants in recent decades.

Assam, however, can ill afford to host these infiltrators; the Assamese population is so small. The recent Citizenship (Amendment) Bill is a major irritant for them especially since what was discovered in 1979. Some young men discovered in the electoral rolls of the Mangaldai assembly constituency that many a voter was an obvious infiltrator. In order to spread the protest and try and stop such distortion of the electoral rolls of the State, the All Assam Students Union (AASU) was formed. Some members also went on to establish the Assam Ganatantra Parishad (AGP), a major political party. A few members took to terrorism under the name of the United Liberation Front of Assam (ULFA).

The Citizenship (Amendment) Bill has understandably upset the people of Assam in the light of the events just narrated. The fear is that many Hindus from Bangladesh may take advantage of this legislation and come over to Assam. Such a legal migration would reduce the percentage of the ethnic Assamese and dilute their indigenous culture. From the viewpoint of illegal infiltration, the Bill is welcome because many of them who came 1971 onwards can be sent back. But many a legal migrant may come in their place. The dilution of the local culture and the threat to the political voice of the Assamese would be about the same. At the same time, we must remember that in 1947 the country was divided on the basis of religion and no other criterion. Pakistan, especially in its western wing, indulged in ethnic cleansing. Today, only three per cent minorities including Christians remain there. The eastern wing had 33 per cent Hindus; only eight per cent now remain. India did not accept Jinnah's two-nation theory and did not do ethnic cleansing. Nevertheless, it cannot forget its duty towards the minorities in Bangladesh or Pakistan. That is the justification of the Citizenship Bill.

The solution to a potentially very serious national problem would lie in making the Cachar district a separate Union Territory having no special political connection with Assam. Cachar has a population of some 40 lakh people of whom a little over half are Hindus; fewer than two per cent are Christians and the rest Muslims. More or less, all of them speak and write Bengali. Its economy is viable especially with the help of over a hundred tea gardens which produce five crore kilograms of tea worth some 800 crore rupees annually. That would separate some 16 per cent of the total Assam population, virtually all of them Bengalis or Muslims—a great relief to the Assamese. A remote possibility perhaps, but the Bodos may also use this as an example and demand a Union Territory of much less than two million people living between Kokrajhar town and Sankosh river to the west. This is the one sure way to bring happiness to the Assamese people after at least a century. In any case, the Cacharis would be pleased at being semi-independent with Silchar becoming a mini *rajdhani*.

Imran's Sanctimoniousness on Minorities

PAKISTAN'S PRIME MINISTER, Imran Khan, has offered to teach India how to treat its minorities. Is it not likely that when he said this, he was experiencing a flashback to his cricketing days, when our fast bowlers were not comparable to his country's pace attack? Traditionally, in the undivided India, it was Punjab that produced pacemen. The one outstanding name that comes to the writer's mind is Mohammad Nissar, the fastest opening bowler that the subcontinent has produced. Certainly, even now, that pack of speed merchants may have something to teach our players.

An Oxonian had once said: Imran is cricket and cricket is Imran. Similarly, Zubin Mehta is music and cannot be imagined in terms of cricket. So, too, it is difficult to reconcile the Imran image with prime ministership. It is possible that while he was talking of minorities, his mind was on how to teach India to play cricket, that too at the Eden Gardens. It goes without saying that he has not seen the holocaust of Hindus and Sikhs starting with Rawalpindi in 1947, nor does he know how his Christian compatriots had rejoiced at the birth of Pakistan only to subsequently regret it, being frequently accused of blasphemy. The Communist Party had wholeheartedly sponsored Partition, later to beat its breast; it was simply eliminated by the torrent of Islam. As late as 2012-13, thirty-seven murderous attacks against people of Christ were reportedly perpetrated. The same year saw sixteen Hindus and three Sikhs bear the brunt of attacks by the zealots of the 'peaceful' religion, who, of course, are committed to cleansing their land of all impurities.

The Ahmadiyyas, whose hero Sir Mohammad Zafarullah Khan had drafted the Pakistan Resolution of March 1940, also had their taste of the glory of Pakistan. Imran Khan was certainly not born then to witness the magnificent work done by Sir Zafarullah; nor when in 1953, when the latter's house in Lahore was set on fire, which induced him to flee Pakistan and not return until his dying days. Zafarullah spent the remainder of his years at The Hague in the Netherlands to bring majesty to the glittering benches of the International Court of Justice. In the meantime, the charismatic Prime Minister, Zulfikar Ali Bhutto, expelled the Ahmadiyyas from the sanctified garden of Islam.

Another Ahmadiyya who brought glory to Imran's country was Dr Abdul Qadeer Khan, whose thuggish doings in the Netherlands enabled him to obtain the secrets of the atomic bomb, all of course in the cause of *Khidmat-e-Allah*—the first Islamic nuclear bomb. He, too, was rewarded by being expelled. Well-known scholar Farahnaz Ispahani in her book *Purifying the Land of the Pure* states the reality of Ahmadiyyas being the target of Pak rulers. As late as 2012-13, according to her book, fifty-four lethal attacks against Ahmadiyyas were carried out.

The author was educated by two men. The first was his grandfather, one of whose friends was Ahmed Ali Jinnah, younger brother of MA Jinnah. He relished Parsi humour and claimed to be culturally a Parsi. Although he was not a practising Muslim, he acquainted my grandfather with his insights into Islam—that when a Muslim wishes to convert someone, it is with the best intention of opening a possible chance of the convert entering *jannat*. Only Allah could enable a non-believer to cross the gateway of heaven.

The second gentleman who taught the author was his Urdu teacher, who did not overtly suggest a conversion but did say that the future lay with Islam. Let us extrapolate the progress of a number of religions. The Yehudis (Jews) have reduced in number and shrunk to a fraction of what they were. The Christians have scattered into many denominations. Many a worshipper in Europe has given up worship. Christianity's priests have come to Asia, where according to the late Pope John Paul-II, there are innumerable souls to harvest. Contrast these performances with the progress of Islam, whose tide is continually rising.

However, all is not well in the new Medina. Once the Ahmadiyyas were expelled from Islam in 1974, it was the turn of the Shias for similar persecution. While they have been the target of the regime's hostility for years, violence against them began rising after the 70s. During 2012-13 alone, they were subjected to 77 attacks, including suicide terrorist bombings during Shia religious observances.

Why to talk only of Shias? The Barelvi school considered

the Deobandis and Wahhabis outside the pale of Islam. They were liable to the death penalty if they fell within the definition *murtad* or apostate. On the other hand, the Justice Munir equality report of 1954 had revealed that a *fatwa* of the Deobandis had called all Asna-Ashari Shias kafirs and *murtad* for believing in the *sahabiyyat* of Hazrat Siddiq-i-Akbar.

In its 2013 annual report, the United States Commission on International Religious Freedom (USCIRF) described Pakistan's failure in protecting its minorities as having reached 'crisis proportions'. According to the report, "The government of Pakistan continues to engage in and tolerate systematic, ongoing, and egregious violations of freedom of religion or belief. Violations reached unprecedented levels", it said, "because of growing incidents of sectarian violence against Shia Muslims". The government also failed to protect the Christians, Ahmadis and Hindus, it said.

In the overall climate of antagonism, Pakistan's blasphemy laws have exacerbated attacks on minorities by fostering religious frenzy, violence and persecution. The police frequently fail to record and investigate complaints, and justice is impeded by the biased attitude of some judges against religious minorities. Pakistan's national discourse, aided by its school curriculum, generates religious prejudice against minorities.

In Pakistan, there are a number of Lashkars (armed militant groups) who are anti-Shia, but the single-minded enemy of the Shias is the Lashkar-e-Jhangvi (LeJ) whose avowed objective is to cleanse Pakistan of them. They incidentally comprise about 20 per cent of the country's population. Balochistan, which has many Shias, is a popular theatre of genocide. The head of the LeJ has gone to the extent of issuing a public letter declaring the Shias to be *wajib-ul-qatl* (ideally suitable for elimination).

Despite this large scale genocide, Pakistan's government has admitted only 2,000 Shias killed over a five-year period.

The Shia-Sunni conflict has a dimension much bigger and beyond the borders of Pakistan. Sunni Saudi Arabia and Shiite Iran are arraigned against each other. Iraq is two-thirds Shia, while the just-ended civil war in Syria was fought between the Shia-sympathetic government and the Caliphate-aspiring ISIS. However, the concern for India is the 25 million Shias in our neighbouring country. If the terrorism becomes collectively unbearable, where do they seek refuge?

Gandhi and Currency Notes

RECENTLY A NIECE, her husband and seven-year-old son Soren stayed with us for a few days. They are citizens of Canada and live in Tornoto. In the course of some payments to a home-delivery Pizza vendor, Soren happened to see several Indian currency notes. Seeing Gandhi's portrait on one he wanted to see all the denominations. To his surprise, he found Gandhi's portrait on each note. Who is this person, he asked me. Why is the great man present on every note? I had said that Gandhi was a saintly man. So the youngster asked, was he so very fond of money that his photograph had to be printed on every bill (as they call notes in America)?

My reply was that he was a saintly man who had little to do with money. He normally lived in an *ashram* or monastery. His great concern was that India should be free from the yoke of the British rule. He wore a simple *dhoti,* and in winter a thin woollen shawl. On his feet he wore *chappals* and generally carried a long bamboo stick to balance himself. He ate simple food and drank goat milk in the morning. You mean, Soren asked, he did not draw even a salary? Who paid for his food? Wherever he lived, he was fed free, I said. You mean he had no money in the bank? No, nothing as far I know, was my reply. Oh my God, exclaimed Soren, you mean your government imposed all this huge collection of bills on him after he died?

I tried to explain to the child that no one has imposed anything on the great man. It is just that the Indian people adore Gandhi so much that they use his portrait on their currency notes. Soren was not satisfied and he went on. Have you no other great man or woman in your country, like they have had so many Presidents in the USA? Every five, ten, twenty or fifty dollar bill has a different portrait. At this point, his father Kevin took over and remarked that our bills did give the impression that Indians were obsessed with Gandhi. Why, after so many years, so many billions are focused on the same person? Hardly any one of you has seen him. And India, from what he had read, had a galaxy of freedom fighters—Nehru, Patel, that soldier hero Subhas and so on.

I replied by saying that if you look at our history, you would find a mega-gallery of great men. A professor who happened to come to the house to visit us joined in to insist that we are being extremely unfair to Gandhi. Money was his last concern, nor was he lucky with wealth. In his days, more Indians walked barefoot than with footwear. More young children walked about half-naked than fully-clothed. We should not involve Gandhi with money, stressed the professor. In fact, he went on, if any of our leaders needs to be remembered for national wealth, it was the late Prime Minister Narasimha Rao who released India from the bondage of socialism and set it free to trade and acquire wealth. Finally, the professor thumped a table nearby and loudly proclaimed that by printing Gandhi on currency notes we were insulting the great old man. And we appear to be hypocritical to the more perceiving when we display Gandhi so much and practice nothing of what he stood for. Lately, we have added a reproduction of his round-frame spectacles on the same currency notes. What do they symbolise, except short-sightedness? What is there to be proud of in that deficiency?

To check on what the young fellow Soren brought up, what I thought and how the professor reacted, I referred the issue to a long-retired but a very wise judge. He was quick to opine. For forty years or so after Independence, we made do with the Ashoka *stambh* or pillar on our notes. There was no human portrait. Then all of a sudden Gandhi's photograph appeared with a vengeance on all denominations. What the provocation was, the judge could not guess. His point was: if the government wanted to spread a noble message or example through the currency, there was a better way.

India has innumerable heroes—ancient, medieval and modern. Why not deploy a separate example with each denomination? Say, Lord Krishna with his insistence on doing one's duty without looking for its reward. And his insistence on the ruler governing for the country and its people and not for himself; Adi Shankaracharya, the father of a great deal of modern Indian thought and spiritual culture; Ramanuja, who propagated *bhakti* through Vedanta; Kabir, with his *sahaja-yoga* or simple union as a secular ideal; Raja Ram Mohan Roy and his anxiety to abolish the evil of *sati*; Swami Vivekananda with his reform of the elimination of child marriage, which is still quite rampant, unfortunately; or his keenness to educate women, his ideals of self perfection and service to society; Sri Aurobindo and his dialectic, cosmic salvation through yoga which transcends reason as well as intuition. Also Netaji Subhas Bose, the hero-soldier of Indian freedom whose Azad Hind Fauj convinced the British that more and more Indians were willing to pick up arms against them; it was, therefore, time for them to leave. Or CV Raman, the Nobel Laureate, for his Raman Effect—change in the wavelength of light that occurs when a light beam is deflected by molecules. Or Gurudev Rabindranath Tagore?

Or say Kalidas and his legendary play *Meghdoot* and others. Or Mirza Asadullah Ghalib, the most popular Urdu poet of the 19th century and his famous words: *Ghalib Ka andaz-e-bayan aur,* or, *Kaabe par purdah bane rehene do ay Ghalib, kahin wahan bhi kafir sanam na nikale.* Or, Rani Ahilya Bai who ruled Indore with distinction for 30 years and built the road that even now links Jagannathpuri to Kolkata. She was the one ruler who replaced many a monumental temple earlier destroyed by foreign invaders including today's Kashi Vishwanath temple and the one at Somnath where the devotees still worship.

Hindu Secularism

JUSTICE SUDIP RANJAN Sen's judgment delivered before the Meghalaya High Court and reported in the press on 13 September 2018 was straightforward—that India should have been declared a Hindu country on the attainment of its independence. For example, until its 1789 Revolution, France had three houses of its National Assembly, one comprising Abbots and Bishops. To go secular, the country had to abolish this third house. Caesar's (ruler's) should be given to him and what is God's should be His. In other words, the 16th century Reformation which became the springboard of secularism or the separation of the Church from the State was, in a way, sanctioned by the Bible. It was, therefore, not difficult to ease out the clergy from the running of government. On the other hand, in an Islamic State, the sovereignty belongs to Allah and not the people. Whatever sweet secular things Jinnah might have said on 11 August 1947 to the Constituent Assembly, the first Constitution of Pakistan attributes sovereignty to Allah.

Let us for a few moments keep aside what Macaulay or English education taught us and consider what the Hindu thinkers thought of their state. The *rajya* or state comprised the monarch whose minimal duties were threefold. He had to defend the borders of the kingdom's territory, to protect the lives and property of his subjects and to appoint a competent *yuvaraj* or successor, not necessarily his son. King Bharat, the forefather of the Kurus had seven sons but he overlooked all of them for not being sufficiently competent. He anointed Bhumanyu who justified his choice. If the monarch wished to go beyond these three duties, it was at his discretion.

The Vedic ethos was current at the time and the elite followed the Sanatan dharma or the eternal faith whose cornerstone was *karma*, leading to *bhagya*, which was the factor of cause and effect. There was no concept of religion and its hierarchies as for example, in Christianity. When Lord Mahavira projected his philosophy called Jainism, it caused no problem. It so happened that when Emperor Chandragupta Maurya decided to retire, he became a Jain *sadhu* and spent the rest of his life around Shravanbelagola in today's Karnataka. There was tolerance of this different viewpoint of how to lead life.

Emperor Ashoka's espousal of Buddhism as his faith and its wherewithal of an organised religion did lead to tensions, especially when he took a lead in preaching Buddhism. For example, he sent his daughter Sanghamitra and his son Mahendra to Sri Lanka. They and their followers converted a large section of the people to Buddhism—people who are now known as Sinhalas. Ashoka sent his missions to many places including Tibet and Asian lands east of India. A monarch turning a proselytizer was against the Hindu way and evoked resistance. The one great saint who led the opposition was Adi Shankaracharya in the eight century. In European terms, this was the first clash between Hinduism and proselytizing insistence upon a particular religious order.

When Islam first came to India, it was confined to Sindh where Muhammad-bin-Qasim won some territory, built a few mosques and converted some people. Nevertheless, it seemed like an episode in isolation, especially in those days when communications were scanty. Mahmud of Ghazni's invasion three centuries later appeared like the adventures of a marauder who was also barbaric. He did butcher people and Hindu priests and destroyed temples but his thrust appeared like that of a powerful robber.

An ongoing trauma settled on the Hindus on the morrow of Muhammad Ghori's conquest of Delhi and his appointment of Qutb-ud-din Aibak to rule from Delhi. With the government authority in the grip of the sultanate, the Hindus, unaccustomed to such brutality, failed to produce an answer. Yes, Maharana Pratap did defend Mewar successfully while Chhatrapati Shivaji demonstrated how Hindus could avenge some of their defeats. Maharaja Ranjit Singh also taught stern lessons to the invaders. But these were three oases in a desert of some 551 years. Even this long desert was interrupted by the East India Company and Robert Clive at the Battle of Plassey in 1775, whereafter Bengal, Bihar and Odisha fell to the British. Hindus had the vicarious satisfaction of the Muslim ruling class tumbling from their thrones and sitting on the same floor. However, it was not a Muslim defeat at Hindu hands.

There is a philosophical block which came in the way of

a Hindu being a ready killer and fighter. A Hindu grows up believing that his salvation lies in his self-actualization through his personal karma; whereas his Muslim counterpart grows up watching animals' throats being cut as the *kalima* is read to make his meat *halal* or permissible. Moreover, as a man he is made to believe that his salvation lies in serving his society, ideally through getting killed in a jihad for the sake of the society. A *shaheed* or such a martyr goes immediately to heaven without waiting years for *qayamat* or doomsday. The Hindu, on the other hand, is told that all living beings are members of his family. So when he kills, he is participating in the homicide of his relative, however distant. In his book *Thoughts on Pakistan* published in 1941, Dr BR Ambedkar endorses MA Jinnah's proposal for Partition of undivided India. His main argument was that it is better to have the enemy outside one's borders than inside. Without being more explicit it was obvious that the two cultures were not naturally congenial, and both would be better off living in separate countries. Jinnah and seven of his leading Muslim League colleagues had wanted an exchange of populations. They wanted Muslims to gather in Pakistan by migrating. Similarly, non-Muslims should vacate the territory of Pakistan.

As distinct from Europe and America, the East has no native concept of the 'secular'. In Arabic, Persian or Urdu, there is no synonym for the word secular. Islam is an all-embracing prescription for life, whether individual or collective, social or political, religious or otherwise. The question of separating any of them does not arise. Hinduism also has no concept of the secular for the simple reason that the Hindu State has never had anything to do with the priest or worship or temple. One synonym for Hinduism is tolerance and another would, in the current context, be secularism. In fact, until Prime Minister Indira Gandhi thrust it during the 1976 Emergency, there was no mention of secularism in our Constitution. The crux of what Justice Sen has asked for is a Hindu, and therefore a tolerant State.

Partition Pangs Persist

THE WRITER HIMSELF has struggled with learning Urdu from two highly-educated Muslim teachers. To that extent, he shares an empathy with the Muslims. He does not mind a Musalman who holds orthodox views and feels that all non-believers are *kafirs*. But then, such a person should undertake a *hijrat* (migration) to a Dar-al-Islam. It is still conveniently possible to emigrate to Pakistan, Bangladesh and a few other countries although the choices have now shrunk.

It is useful to know the brief background of this problem. Upon Partition, the Muslims left behind in India were understandably apprehensive. MA Jinnah and seven other senior colleagues had proposed an exchange of populations. According to this scheme, the Hindus should do their best to vacate Pakistan whereas the Muslims in Hindustan would leave India for the newly-found Pakistan. Those unable to move could stay back and in the words of Jinnah, "continue to reside as reciprocal hostages". Dr Rajendra Prasad, India's first president for twelve years, in his book *India Divided* published in 1946, recommended that those minorities who stayed back would reside as aliens who were issued visas. Those who heard these suggestions of the two big leaders became even more apprehensive. Jinnah's attitude was harsh. He was leaving the Imperial Hotel Delhi for the airport to depart for Karachi, in order to deliver his inaugural speech to the Constituent Assembly. It is alleged that a small group of Muslims had come to meet their leader. To them Jinnah said: "You have done nothing to win Pakistan. I alone have achieved the new country."

As it happened, Jawaharlal Nehru did not have an adequate support base in the Congress Party. When in 1946, the party office enquired as was the procedure for electing a new president, 15 Pradesh Congress Committees opted for Sardar Patel, while one PCC chose Acharya JB Kripalani; none voted for Nehru. Yet, Gandhi insisted on appointing his favourite Nehru through the 21-member Working Committee of the party. The party president would automatically take over as the vice-president of the Interim Government, when it was formed later the same year and then eventually be the prime minister of India. Nehru's support base was still missing. The traumatised Muslims left in India were his sitting ducks for acquiring a base. Most of them remained his supporters throughout. The general impression has been that almost 90 per cent of Muslims vote and, therefore, are a valuable base. This was the secret behind the Muslims acquiring and holding (until 2014), a veto on Indian policy—whether overturning through Parliament the Supreme Court granting Shah Bano a deserved alimony because it was against the Sharia, or Dr Manmohan Singh, former Prime Minister, declaring "Muslims First" and "fifteen per cent of the country's resources to be given to the Muslims first".

Since 2014, the perception of the Hindus has changed. They feel that 'enough is enough'. They would now like to enjoy their freedom after these seven decades, without causing inconvenience to anyone else. The Shias have recognised the change in perception and opted out of the Ayodhya fray. The Sunnis are holding out but to what benefit, only they know. Is it worth waging a tussle for a small piece of land? Do they realise how they are hurting the 'believing' Hindus?

The only criterion on which British India was divided was religion and none other. It was certainly not on territorial grounds as Gandhi told Syama Prasad Mookerjee in the presence of Dr Rajkumari Amrit Kaur in January 1948. Thirty per cent of the land was allotted by the departing British government for 25 per cent of the people which was then the total Muslim population. With a third of the Muslims staying behind, the land allocation to Pakistan was in excess.

If an exchange of population had taken place, the demographic picture of India would have been very different. As it happened, West Pakistan drove out nearly all its Hindus and Sikhs; whereas, comparatively very few Muslims emigrated from India. East Pakistan (now Bangladesh) has over a period of years pushed out three-fourths of its Hindus. Thus Pakistan and Bangladesh have grabbed more than their fair share of the land area. From every angle, the obligation to adjust amicably rests with the Muslims who have stayed back in India just as the Christians, Parsis and Jews lead a congenial life. They create no tensions and certainly no riots whereas Hindu-Muslim riots take place somewhere or the other with the regularity of the annual *shraddha* for praying to Hindu ancestors! Gandhi had said at the Round Table Conference in 1931 that such riots were coeval with the British rule and would cease when the British departed. How many riots have taken place since Independence and how many lives lost? Was he talking utter baloney? Or did he not have sense enough to know that before the British, the Muslims ruled in many parts of the country? How could there be riots between the rulers and the ruled?

Articles 25 and 30 of the Constitution placed the minorities superiorly whereas the majority community has lesser rights. Moreover, they contradict Article 14, which guarantees equality before the law to all citizens of India. They also directly negate Article 15, which is meant to ensure all citizens against discrimination, whether in matters of religion or any other. Articles 25 to 30, therefore, need to be abrogated.

India would have been a rather different country had it not been saddled with a 50-year rule by Aurangzeb in the seventeenth century. There would have been no temple desecration, no reintroduction of the *jaziya* tax and other oppressions against the Hindus. As a contrast, had Shah Jahan's eldest son Dara Shikoh become the emperor instead of Aurangzeb, India would most likely have not been divided into Hindustan and Pakistan.

Muslims and Inclusiveness

THERE IS NO doubt that the Muslims, especially the Sunnis, are experiencing some fear as to what would happen next. Until 2014, more or less, the Nehruvian ethos prevailed. Most political parties chased the Muslim vote because the community patronised the polling booth more seriously than the others. The decade of 2004-2014 especially favoured the community because the then Prime Minister Manmohan Singh went on repeating "Muslims First" and saying that 15 per cent of the country's resources would be allocated to them first. In any case, they or their clergy held the veto over Indian policy. Notwithstanding what the Constitution has recommended, there was no attempt to move towards a Uniform Civil Code. The Rajiv Gandhi government had the temerity to overturn the Supreme Court judgement granting alimony to a poor widow named Shah Bano in 1986.

Then suddenly Mr Narendra Modi was elected with a clear majority in the Lok Sabha. He declared 'justice for all and appeasement of none' which came as a surprise. It came as a shock to the secular media and the entire Lutyens type elite in every city which was united against Modi. To add to that, screen giants like Amir Khan and Shah Rukh Khan expressed a feeling of insecurity. The former even talked of emigrating. Life, however, went on as usual. There were very few riots in the course of five years.

When the 2019 elections neared, even the TV channels sympathetic to the BJP predicted a hung Lok Sabha with 200 to 220 seats to this party. Some journalists commented that at 200, the BJP itself may throw up alternative PM candidates. Such predictions were a balm to the Muslims as well as the secularists. Over and above, as the campaign began all opposition parties said that their central objective was to defeat Modi. All these mountains of hope crashed as election results were announced on 23 May. The shock must have been felt by nearly everyone.

The Muslims were confused by the circumstances when Partition took place. On one hand, the Muslim League leaders kept repeating through 1946 and 1947 that they insisted on emigration of Muslims from Hindustan and of Hindus and Sikhs from what would be Pakistan. In other words, they favoured an exchange of populations. Dr BR Ambedkar had supported the idea as early as 1941, whereas Dr Rajendra Prasad, later president of India, proposed another alternative in his book called *India Divided*. According to him, those Muslims who did not emigrate should be allowed to stay in India as aliens with the help of visas.

Justice Gopal Das Khosla ICS, was commissioned soon after the Partition to survey the Punjab and report what was happening there. In a book containing his survey called *Stern Reckoning*, he stated that an exchange of populations was integral to the partition. MA Jinnah, in his 22 March 1940 speech recommending the passing of the Pakistan Resolution by the League, had lucidly explained how and why Hindus and Muslims could not coexist in one country. All these were high level exchanges of ideas and proposals. The common folk were unaware of them. Once the western wing of Pakistan had been cleared of most Hindus and Sikhs and the process had also begun in the eastern wing, the Muslim leaders went cold on their own earlier proposals. The Hindus in Hindustan did not resort to the scale of violence witnessed in Punjab; and not many Muslims chose to migrate but remained in Hindustan.

Although he had become prime minister, Jawaharlal Nehru had no base in his Congress party. In 1946, the vote of 16 Pradesh Congress Committees was taken as to whom they would prefer as the next party president. Fifteen supported Sardar Vallabhbhai Patel and one preferred Acharya JB Kripalani. None mentioned Nehru. Yet, because of Gandhi's partiality, Nehru was forced on the party through an irregular appointment by the twenty-one member Working Committee.

After Partition became a reality, many a Muslim would have felt apprehensive, if not actually traumatised. Jawaharlal had once boasted that he was a Muslim by culture, English by upbringing and Hindu by accident. The post-Partition Muslims supported Nehru to become their leader. In return, he obliged them with Articles 25 to 30 in the Constitution, especially 29 and 30, which gave the minorities rights superior to the majority. The Christians had no difficulty in setting up schools, nor did they need subsidies from the government. In this context, therefore, the word 'minority' was and continues to be treated as a polite euphemism for Muslims. This is how the foundations were laid for the Muslim clergy to acquire a veto on Indian policy, for example as demonstrated by the Muslim Women's Bill of 1986. The clergy, in turn, returned the favour by inducing its followers to vote solidly. This vote was invaluable, especially in the years when the Hindus were indifferent and only about 35 to 40 per cent of them visited the polling booths. Finally, Dr Manmohan Singh and his "Muslims First" policy awakened the Hindus, an awakening that helped bring Narendra Modi to power in 2014.

The Muslim community also had its own compulsions. For example, no emphasis was placed on education, especially for women. Debate was not encouraged, although at the level of the clergy, *ijtihad* (reinterpretation) was permitted in the initial centuries of Islam. But for a thousand years now, it has been discouraged and emphasis has been laid on *taqlid* (orthodoxy). For many centuries bygone, the Muslim women have been looked upon as a source of service, pleasure and procreation. All these factors are today out of step with modernity, but in a man's world, they were the secret of Islam's growth. The late Syed Shahabuddin IFS, also a Member of Parliament in his days, used to repeatedly say that for Muslims, identity was more important than development. Business and industry have not been encouraged by the Islamic ethos. For example, charging interest is considered *haram*. Yet, those sections of Muslims who were converted in the last few centuries like the Bohras, Memons and Khojas are successful at business. On the average, the Muslims in Gujarat are quite prosperous.

Due to the challenge to its identity, the community has

made no noticeable attempt to identify itself with the Indian ethos. Many an Islamic country has reformed its personal laws. Even in Pakistan, polygamy is not permitted; a man cannot take a second wife without satisfying the district magistrate that doing so is essential for him. The Sharia is a product of the Holy Quran, but then why only the personal law? Why not also its criminal law? Why is the Indian Penal Code welcome when it comes to punishing crime? The obstinacy of the community's leadership drove Javed Akhtar and Ms Shabana Azmi to once say that a uniform civil code was the only salvation for the Muslim woman.

Islam considers it not right for a Muslim to be a citizen of a country dominated by *kafirs* or non-believers. British rule was permissible because they were '*Ahl-e-Kitab*' (People of the Book). Hindus are non-believers and, therefore, in a democratic polity it becomes a Dar-al-Harb (land of conflict). The British period was described by Sir Syed Ahmed Khan as Dar-ul-Aman (land of peace). India was recognied as Dar-al-Islam until the Mughals ruled. In this context, the aware Muslim may be feeling entrapped by having to live in India, even more so when the BJP is in power. The fact that hardly any person in Gujarat has been killed since 2002 (the riots at the time were provoked by setting fire to a train coach at Godhra), makes little difference.

Why and how Partition occurred has never been explained to the common folk. Dr Rafiq Zakaria, an eminent Muslim scholar-cum-politician of Maharashtra, has squarely blamed Jinnah for the division of the country. In the name of 'Islam in danger' the Qaid-e-Azam sold the dream of a new Medina.

There is a delusion around Ayodhya. Most Hindus believe that Lord Rama was born where Mir Baqi built a *masjid* without a minaret, or a maqbara for himself. Poet Allama Iqbal had called Sri Rama *Imam-e-Hind.* Surely some leaders could have risen to pay a tribute to the Hindu sentiment by letting go of the area rather than fighting over it for years in the Supreme Court. The Shias have shown this grace. It would have been a tribute also to Hindus not having raised the issue of 3,000 odd temples that have been converted in the past into mosques. This underlines the challenge of inclusiveness before the country.

One Nation, One Poll

ONE NATION, ONE election is not only an appealing call but also a pragmatic one. Indeed, this was the practice until the 1967 general elections. With the Congress party being the dominant political factor, no objection was raised. Thereafter, in a number of States there were defections from the Congress. New parties came into being and governments were formed by them; for example, Chaudhary Charan Singh left the grand old party and formed the Samyukta Vidhayak Dal government in UP. The uniform five-yearly pattern of polls was disturbed. After the 1972 Lok Sabha 'Garibi Hatao' election, several state governments were dismissed under section 356 which also led to out-of-turn polls without maintaining any uniformity of pattern.

Now that there are a number of parties, most of them regional formations, there are likely to be some objections to simultaneous polls. There is no doubt that frequent elections, whether in one state or the other, make life continually preoccupied with campaigning. As a result, there remains less time and energy for the politicians to concentrate on governance. Polls are merely the means for selecting governments and not an end in themselves. But with frequent elections, the means tend to become the end and the end is reduced to being incidental. Moreover, populism is thrust upon the parties for fear of losing votes. For truly national parties, continual elections are a punishment without having committed any crime. Campaigning becomes like a continual marriage celebration for a family—all celebrations and no normal life. For the party in power at New Delhi, continual campaigning not only means continued stress but depriving governance of its full attention. Plus, its policies could get coloured by populism in order not to lose votes. Populism is an enemy of development. For the country, frequent elections mean an enormous financial burden. For the people, it means higher taxes or greater inflation.

There is a flip side to this list of disadvantages of frequent polling. Take the Bangladesh War of 1971; India's quick victory and Pakistan's total humiliation had a decisive impact on the 1972 general election. The cause of Indira Gandhi's triumph had less to do with Garibi Hatao and more to do with Pakistan being cut into half. Incidentally, Hindus are perpetually hungry for victories because they have experienced no triumph over a foreign power since Chandragupta Maurya expelled Seleucus from India nearly 2,400 years ago. Any wonder that Indians delight at a Test cricket victory and go delirious when we defeat Pakistan? The 2019 Balakot airstrike in March had greater influence on the 2019 general election than the Delhi elite realise.

Imagine, a one nation, one poll for the regional parties or even a national opposition party in the foreground of a military victory. Except for the cool, calm and thinking voter, any national triumph would influence a normally emotional voter. A person who votes for the central party is also likely to cast his mandate for the same party in the state. If pleased with a state leader, he is also likely to support the party's Lok Sabha candidate. There might not have been many charismatic state leaders whereby the central vote could be diverted. Nevertheless, state causes or grievances like the Kaveri water dispute or Hindi language could influence voting.

The thrust of this finding is that while commending the reduction of electioneering and consolidating polls, the Central and the Sates hustings should be held separately. The 2014 and 2019 central polls were held in the month of May. All the states together can go to elect their governments in say, November. This would confine the poll season to only twice in five years. If any government were to fall mid-term, every attempt should be made to reconstitute it. If that is not possible, the state concerned would have to bear with governor's rule until the five years are over. The re-election should take place along with the rest of the states. If the central government were to fall and could not be re-formed, there would be no alternative to a mid-term poll.

Another electoral issue repeatedly raised by lady legislators, and promptly swept under the carpet by male members is with regard to reservations for women in Parliament. There are several castes and communities which by tradition do not wish to accept women as equal. Their arguments are several. One of them is that reservation, if given, would benefit the more fashionable women while the traditional or conservative would be left out. The chances of men being given tickets and getting elected would be reduced by up to one-third. It is also true that not a sufficient number of women have rubbed shoulders with common folk. To that extent, not many have yet qualified to be candidates. There can be no limit to excuses when the implementers are unwilling.

When the first general election was held in 1952, the population was around 30 or 32 crores. Today the numbers are estimated to be 130 crores or about four times. The number of representatives in the Lok Sabha has not been increased commensurately. In other words, there is scope for an increase.

There are constitutions, like in Germany, that provide for the contesting political parties to *nominate* a percentage of those numbers who have been elected in the public elections. For example, Parliament could consider organising an institute of training future legislators so that the candidates for nominations know the Constitution plus essential facts about the country, and the rules and procedures of the conduct of Parliament proceedings.

A dose of public speaking could be added so that members do not have problems of expressing themselves in Hindi or English. When the writer was a member, making one's speech meant spoken and not read. It appears that this restraint has lately been relaxed; it should not be. Incidentally, very seldom is the Lok Sabha fully attended. Most of the time the house is more empty than full, especially in the afternoons. On peak days, the House of Commons at Westminster is so chock-a-block that a few members have to stand.

Mandir-Masjid Syndrome

REPORTS THAT SOME forty-nine temples have been built on government land in a single Delhi parliamentary constituency are unfortunate. If these reported encroachments are true, the government must deal with them accordingly. If neglected for too long chances are the issue could take on a communal hue. There are some three thousand temples across the country which were in the centuries past converted into mosques. Not all of them may remain dead issues. No government has taken the trouble to solve them and they have been left to be settled judicially. In course of time, such issues turn into political controversies. The self-styled secular parties would be reluctant to offend their Muslim constituents whereas others would need to assuage their Hindu followers.

Take Ayodhya and the Ramjanmabhoomi controversy,

which has reached the heights of absurdity. There has never been any doubt about who brought down the mandir, replaced it with a structure and when. He was Mir Baqi in about 1530 AD. The edifice was without a minaret or a *wuzoo*, very unusual for a mosque. Responsible Muslims avoid praying in edifices that were earlier used by non-believers for their worship. In all probability, this structure at Ayodhya was a *maqbara* or mausoleum for Babar or for Mir Baqi. Down the ages, someone must have called it a mosque and so it became one. At some stage, the Shias lost interest and the local Sunnis took over. Lately, the head of the Shia Personal Law Board, Janaab Rizvi, has declared that his community wishes Hindus to build a temple there if they like. The Shias no longer lay any claim to it. On the other hand, the Sunni Personal Law Board is fighting the case in the Supreme Court with a do or die determination. What does Sunni Personal Law have to do with a Shia stone structure, whatever it might have been?

It is not widely realised that this conflict going on and on is a price paid by our democracy. For fear of losing votes, politicians avoid dealing decisively with such issues preferring the judiciary to handle them. When in the 1930s Sir Sikandar Hayat Khan was the Premier of Punjab, the High Court decided a case favouring the Sikhs to retain the Shahidganj edifice as a gurdwara although it was earlier a masjid. The popular Muslim reaction was that the verdict was unfair and the government should go in appeal to the Privy Council in London and get back their place of worship. Sir Sikandar declined to appeal. The reason he gave was that if all the temples converted into mosques in the rest of India, especially Ajmer Sharif, were to win in the Privy Council, all these mosques would have to be returned. This was decisive statesmanship, despite its potential unpopularity.

Sir Arnold Toynbee, the distinguished British historian, associated a place of worship with national honour when in 1960 he came to Delhi to deliver the Maulana Azad Memorial Lecture. He expressed great surprise at Aurangzeb's mosque at Varanasi still standing. He felt that it should have been removed and illustrated the issue with a Polish example. In 1817, when the Russians conquered Warsaw, they converted the city's main church from a Catholic to an Orthodox place of worship, merely to humiliate the Poles. When in 1918, Russia had lost in World War I and Poland became independent, the Poles retaliated by demolishing the Orthodox church and replacing it with a Roman Catholic one. That was for national honour, said Toynbee.

To take an Indian example, Sardar Vallabhbhai Patel visited Junagadh on 12 November 1947, as a mark of celebration for the people of Saurashtra having recovered the princely state of Junagadh from the jaws of Pakistan. The Sardar had the humiliation of the Somnath temple on his mind. In the afternoon, he visited the Veraval beach where the original temple of Somnath was situated. The current temple was a modest one, built at the behest of Maharani Ahilyabai of Indore. Patel, having had a darshan, went on to decide to build a grand temple of Lord Shiva nearby. He appealed to the public to donate funds and to the government to have the mandir built under the direction of Kanaiyalal Munshi, a Cabinet colleague as well as an outstanding Gujarati litterateur. The project was completed in 1951 and to the exasperation of Prime Minister Nehru, Rashtrapati Rajendra Prasad agreed to inaugurate the new Somnath temple.

So far, governments in India have been turning a deaf ear and a blind eye to issues relating to places of worship, especially mandirs and masjids. This has been a policy of escapism in order not to risk losing votes. This, however, is wrong; it is the duty of the state to resolve such issues in a rightful manner. It is, therefore, suggested that, without interfering with worship or religion, the government concerned should take hold of any controversy and give an early decision in an impartial manner, so that disputes do not turn into communal conflicts and eventually develop into political opportunities.

Relevant in this context would be the Places of Worship Act 1991, which was tailor-made for mischief. It was passed during the monsoon session of Parliament a year earlier in preparation for the Babri demolition. The moot point that this legislation made was that no place of worship could be changed from the shape or form it was in at the time of Independence but with one exception—namely, the Babri edifice at Ayodhya, which could be altered as was implied in the Act.

On 6 December 1992, the motive behind the Act could be seen clearly. When darkness fell on Ayodhya, by 5.30 pm, the Babri building had not fallen; only the three domes had crashed. Uncannily, no photograph of this scene, the building without the domes, has been available anywhere. By 5.45 pm, four BJP state governments had been dismissed. The UP governor was in charge of the State at Lucknow. UP, after 5.45 pm was in the hands of the Central government. At 10 pm, Prime Minister Narasimha Rao in a television speech condemned the demolition at Ayodhya and promised that the masjid would be rebuilt. In actual fact, all that was necessary was to reconstruct the three domes.

By the morning of 9 December, there was not a sign left of the erstwhile edifice. Ram Lalla's *murti* (icon) had taken its place in a tent temple. What was uncanny earlier in the day of 6 December was the thrashing received by several press photographers. These young men had thought that they were going to project the Kar Sevaks by photographing them. Instead, the Sevaks asked them to stop photographing and surrender their camera films. When the photographers did not comply, their cameras were snatched and the men were beaten black and blue. Normally, the Kar Sevaks should have been appreciative of being photographed, but in this instance, they were antagonistic. The question is whether they had any official connection with the demolition and whether their photographs could compromise their positions.

On 25 March 2020, the idols of Ram Lalla were shifted from the tent in *garbha griha* (sanctum sanctorum) to a temporary temple near Manas Bhawan, 250m away from the old tented temple made after the demolition of the Babri mosque on 6 December 1992. The issue was finally resolved when a bench of Supreme Court headed by former Chief Justice of India Ranjan Gogoi ruled in favour of the Hindus. The Muslims were given land separately for the construction of a mosque.

Partition and Hindus

IT DOES NOT matter who precisely initiated the move for Partition. For one, it took place seven decades ago. For another, most Hindus appeared to be unhappy about it; indeed, many still yearn for Akhand Bharat. A few Hindu organisations still express regret collectively on 14 August every year. Some Muslims began voicing regret at the division after 1971 when Pakistan was bifurcated. With it came the realisation that perhaps Islam was not sufficient to hold a country together. Otherwise, Muslims in India, who gained nothing from the Partition, would also have drawn satisfaction from having created a New Medina, a large Dar-al- Islam on the subcontinent.

There is no doubt that Vinayak Damodar Savarkar differentiated between Hindus and those whose *punyabhoomi* or holy land was overseas. There could be other contemporaries who felt similarly but did not record their ideological views. Dr BR Ambedkar was different in this regard. He was clear and lucid when he wrote that he did not wish to end his life as a Hindu. When he considered Christianity and Islam, he promptly rejected them on the ground that they would denationalise his people because of their foreign roots. Moreover, converting to Islam would add to the number of Muslims, who, he felt, tended to be separatist. More Christians, Ambedkar believed would increase support for the British rulers who were Christian. He, therefore, turned to Buddhism. In his book titled *Thoughts on Pakistan* published in 1941, he supported Partition which the Muslim League had demanded by passing a resolution in its plenary session held at Lahore in March 1940.

The first leader to declare that Hindus and Muslims were separate nations was Sir Syed Ahmad Khan, who was a member of the Viceroy's Executive Council and the founder of the Aligarh Muslim University. His statement of separate nations was voiced twice; once at Meerut in 1887 and again at Lucknow the following year. Justice Ameer Ali of Calcutta had endorsed Sir Syed's opinion at the turn of the 19th century. In 1906, Sir Aga Khan had led a delegation of thirty-five Muslim eminences to petition before Viceroy Lord Minto. They had three demands: one, recognition of Aligarh as a Muslim University, although it had been wholly funded by the government; two, they wanted reservations for Muslims in government services and three; no elections but nominations instead. They found it difficult to compete with Hindus because of their few numbers and lesser English education. The same year in December, the Muslim League was founded at Dacca. The Morley Minto Reforms or the Indian Councils Act of 1909 was the outcome. The first demand regarding Aligarh was not conceded but the remaining two were a part of the new law.

The next significant step in the pathway to Partition was the Muslim League session at Allahabad in 1930. Sir Muhammad Iqbal, the distinguished poet presided over the session and proposed a separate Muslim zone, although within the Indian confederation. It is believed that Jinnah drew inspiration from Allama Iqbal, although in his eventual demand Bengal as well as Assam were included. In 1933, Choudhry Rahmat Ali, a scholar at the University of Cambridge coined the word 'Pakistan' using letters from some of the Muslim dominated provinces. He published a pamphlet *Now or Never; Are We to Live or Perish Forever?* This new name kept the gossip propelled until eventually in March 1940 Jinnah delivered his long speech justifying the League demand for Pakistan. This was followed the next day on 23 March by the actual resolution proposed by Fazlul Haque, a Muslim Bengali statesman and jurist.

Surprisingly, Muslim majority provinces like Punjab, Bengal, North West Frontier and Sind did not show much enthusiasm. They might have been happy as they were with the Muslims dominating the provinces, also with Muslim premiers. On the other hand, it was UP, Bihar and the business interests of Bombay who were the vanguard of the movement. Interestingly, Ratilal Gandhi, a relative of the writer, then president of Bombay PCC, once had a discussion with one Habib, the head of the group which went on in Pakistan to set up the Habib Bank as well as industries. Ratilal wanted to know why the Habibs were financing the League when all the group's business and property were only around Bombay. Habib replied that in Bombay, he had to complete with Marwaris, Parsis, other banias, Shettys, perhaps even Chettiars, etc. In Pakistan he would have only the Punjabi peasants as his rivals.

Numerous Aligarh University students went to Punjab to campaign for the Muslim League during the 1945-46 elections called by the British government. The Leagues' sole agenda was Partition. Curious Punjabis asked them why they had come all the way from UP. What did they have at stake? Their province (UP) wouldn't be included in Pakistan. The UP students invariably replied that while it was true they personally had no direct interest, but for Islam, they might succeed in creating a New Medina, i.e., a model Islamic state. Quite possibly UP and Bihar were influenced by such an ideal.

Jinnah had explained to the senior members of the League the reasons for seeking Pakistan. In India, Muslims are in a minority and less educated in the modern sense. The elite of the community were mostly land and property owners with very little business and industry, which the Hindus had. Therefore, Muslims would be at a disadvantage all the way. Hence, they needed their homeland. Being a lawyer and a clear-headed thinker, Jinnah had a plan for an exchange of populations; most Muslims would relocate to Pakistan while Hindus and Sikhs would migrate to Hindustan. Those who could not move would have to stay put, but as reciprocal hostages. Dr Rajendra Prasad, our first Rashtrapati, in his book *India Divided* published in 1946 added to Jinnah's proposition that those who stayed back should live as aliens with visas issued by the respective central governments. But Gandhi and Nehru turned a deaf ear to these proposals and the monstrous riots followed.

Fascism is Class Collaboration

HARDLY A WEEK passes without the Pakistani Prime Minister Imran Khan accusing India of being fascist. Even Indian politicians are not discriminating in their use of the world. The author has enquired of several students of political science the meaning of the word but has not found a satisfactory answer. "Despotic", "ruthless" were the off-the-cuff explanations. Textbooks on the science have not thought it necessary to include a chapter on fascism. As a practitioner of fascism, Adolf Hitler is usually the first name on people's lips. Benito Mussolini is a poor second.

What everyone does not realise is that the word is not a political abuse that they think it is. Benito Mussolini, who initiated the Fascist movement in March 1919 at Milan and founded the party called Partito Nazionale Fascista in

November 1921, eventually died in defeat and disgrace. That is, however, too far-fetched to be abusive. Or, does the very word "fascist" denote political derogation? Perhaps it does to at least some members of the Indian intelligentsia. This is reason enough to recapitulate what was fascism.

The word "fascio" means a bundle or a bunch implying unity. The movement was in response to the corruption, unemployment and the virtual economic collapse in Italy after World War I. The socio-economic conditions appeared to be ripe for a socialist revolution and fascism was a nationalist answer to pre-empt a communist takeover. Marxism was looked upon as depicting "class conflict". Capitalism still carried the stigma of "class exploitation" and was therefore a non-starter as a popular programme. To be effective, the answer had to be something that would prove attractive to the peasants, to the workers, as well as to their unions. This was discovered in "class collaboration" as represented by fascism.

Prof Alfredo Rocco, the Minister of Justice in the Mussolini cabinet, set forth the gist of this new ideology in the course of a speech at Perugia in 1925. According to him, society does not exist for the individual; the individual exists for the society. Economic progress is a social interest and all classes of people should combine or collaborate to maximise production. The interests of the employers and the employed are identical. To ensure that this is practised, there must be a system of state discipline over class conflicts. Strikes and lockouts were alike illegal and punishable by heavy fines and in certain cases by imprisonment.

Wherever possible, the employers and workers in each industry, trade or profession were organised together in syndical associations. Where it was not possible to form such syndicates, the unions and the employers' associations remained, but combined to form guilds to coordinate and ensure cordiality. If collective bargaining could not end satisfactorily, the disputes were referred to law courts assisted by experts. This is how class collaboration was conceptualised by the Fascist Party.

In practice, the economy was toned up by rearmament and public works. Soldiers were recruited in large numbers and so were workers in factories to produce arms. This would bring profits to the bourgeoisie who could then pay the proletariat well. Urban prosperity would increase demand for agricultural produce. What was left of the under-employed youth was absorbed by the armed forces. The promise to the whole nation was foreign conquests, which would bring booty. The Albanian adventure and the invasion of Abyssinia were two efforts to fulfil this promise, until of course World War II took place.

Another example of the practice of fascism or class collaboration, albeit on a much more limited scale, was in Spain under General Franco. Neither the Italian nor the Spanish experience is widely known in any great detail in India. What, however, the members of the intelligentsia are familiar with are the exploits of Adolf Hitler and his Nazi Party, whose full name was National Socialist German Workers' Party. It was founded by Hitler and his six comrades in Munich in 1920. The economic deprivation in Germany was much greater than witnessed in Italy. The country paid an exorbitant price for its defeat in World War I. The runaway inflation, as well as the world depression ignited by the crash in share prices on the Wall Street in New York in 1929, made matters hot for Germany. It was widely believed that the charismatic genius of Hitler and his programme of class collaboration, more or less on the lines of Mussolini's Italy, although on a far grander scale, saved the country from utter collapse and a communist takeover.

Unlike the Italian and Spanish examples, the Nazi Party proposed to exclude Jews from German life. They alleged that the Jewish leadership had betrayed the state during World War I and was to a large extent responsible for the German defeat. In their bid to exterminate the Jews, not only from Germany but also from the rest of Europe, the Nazis were estimated to have killed six million Jews by 1945. While General Franco confined himself to Spain, Benito Mussolini did attempt foreign conquests but his plans were nowhere as grandiose as Adolf Hitler's. This is why he is also well-known not only in India but the world over.

So much for fascism and its smaller as well as grander (Spanish and German) variations. But what is its ugly connection with politics in India? India is not Europe and the 2020s are not the 1930s. Socialism is on its deathbed and there is no fear of a communist takeover in India. There is economic deprivation but there is no financial collapse on the scale of pre-Hitler Germany. Indian ethos has no record of imperialism and, therefore, no promise of foreign conquests that would be credible. If an attempt is being made to compare the Jews of Germany and the Muslims of India, it is ridiculous. No one has accused the Muslims of betraying India, not even the BJP whose only contention is that there has been appeasement of Muslim whims and pampering of the community's leadership. All in all, to call anyone a fascist in India is to talk nonsense.

Sustaining a National Party

IF ANYONE WISHES to establish a new political outfit or revive an old one, he/she must have a quasi-federal plan. A fundamental reason is that Indians vote according to the leader they trust most or distrust least. They are not guided very much by the manifesto or the ideology beyond it. That is why parties are seldom particularly punctual in respect of distributing their pre-electoral manifestos; not infrequently only a few days before polling. The parties know that they are performing merely a formality and not a necessity.

Every democrat agrees that there should be one or two national-scale opposition parties. There are many who believed that the Congress was the right one but it is doddering. In the opinion of the writer, it is revivable as it has an enormous brand equity built up over 130 years. At the same time, there is a scope in our vast country to build up another party as well. There is plenty of talent; imagine most of the latent political energies of women are yet untapped.

The result is that the leaders need to be charismatic or attractive or at least identifiable. Such leaders find it easier to rise in the States than at the national level. This is not a new phenomenon; it is as old as the Nehru years when he was the prime minister. Almost every province or state had a leader from the Congress or from any other party. Assam had Gopinath Bordoloi, West Bengal had the combination of Bidhan Chandra Roy and Atulya Ghosh, Bihar had Shri Krishna Sinha and Dr Anugrah Narayan Sinha, Orissa had Harekrishna Mahtab and later Biju Patnaik, Madras had K Kamaraj and C Rajagopalachari, and Kerala had Pattom Thanu Pillai and later Manakkal Sankaran Namboodiripad. Maharashtra or Bombay had BG Kher and later Yashwantrao Chavan, Rajasthan had Mohan Lal Sukhadia, Punjab, Pratap Singh Kairon, UP had Govind Vallabh Pant while Central Provinces (now MP) was led by Pandit Ravi Shankar Shukla and Karnataka had S Nijalingappa. Jawaharlal Nehru, after the death of Vallabhai Patel, enjoyed the federal leadership of the Congress unchallenged. His monopoly remained secure despite the Kashmir syndrome and the mistakes he made in his China policy. Surprisingly, no rival of a national stature came up until his death in 1964. His successor was Lal Bahadur Shastri who was until then a political lightweight. Thereafter came the long reign of Indira Gandhi in the course of which all federalism, except that formally written in the Constitution, virtually ended.

The Emergency is unforgettable. Earlier when Indira left the Congress in 1969, nearly all the property that the party owned was left behind with the Syndicate faction. She did not replace any or hire many premises. Half of the District Congress Committees worked out of the local presidents' homes. The West Bengal Pradesh Congress Committee functioned from 250 Chittaranjan Avenue, Ajit Panja's residence. Indira Gandhi apparently worked on the theory of her charisma and her admiring voters with the party men being unpaid workers. This is merely to illustrate the contrast between the federal working in Nehru's time and the autocratic functioning in his daughter's time. If a national opposition party is to be built up, the federal style would have to be adopted. The regional leaders would then get their importance and be the pillars of the central dome. They would not be mere branch managers who could be appointed or removed at the sweet will of the monarch in New Delhi.

Since the time of Nehru, a new problem has developed; that is of money. Earlier each Pradesh Congress Committee raised its own funds locally. With the progress of time, politicians have come to believe that money is the petrol that runs elections. Every state is not rich enough to provide funds on a large scale. Money has then got to be given by the High Command. 'He who pays the piper calls the tune' principle willy-nilly begins to operate. A national party must, therefore, create a reasonable minimum fund centrally rather in the manner of conservative parties in Europe. The distribution of money should then be either on the basis of state population or any other formula so that there is no piper who can call the tune arbitrarily. Above all, there has got to be the determination of members not to allow anyone to become the owner of a party that aspires to be national. That does not mean that there would be no ownership parties. There would be, but then their future can only be of a substitute. When, in an election, the voters do not want to elect the party in power, they may have to vote for an ownership organization. However, when there is a choice of an alternative national party, there would be no need to vote for a proprietary set-up. In principle, there should be nothing objectionable about an ownership party. The only question is—does it not discourage competent individuals from coming into political life? Not everyone can bow to the proprietors or flatter them to gain favours like being given a ticket to contest a poll.

There are few things worse for a society than to be landed with a poor government. The Westminster Parliamentary system especially needs voters to be careful and cautious. Persons who get elected to become lawmakers can end up becoming ministers who ideally must be first-rate executives. Often the prime minister does not have a free choice. He has to ensure that all possible sections of the people are represented in the ministry. Not everyone can be a first-rate executive. In contrast, the American Presidential system challenges voters to elect an excellent president. He/she can take care of the quality of all other appointments. Our fellow citizens need to be reminded of these factors. The reason is that statesmanship does not come naturally to even the Indian elite, what to speak of the common folk. Most of our country has been ruled for centuries by foreigners.

What was the level of our people's interest in politics is difficult to tell. Historically, there was very little literature on the subject. The ancient eras of India gave forth treasures of philosophy and history,which can be considered the mother of political science. Yet, other than the *Arthashastra,* nothing has been on the known horizon. Only recently there appeared a volume called *Krishna Rajya.* Does this paucity not reflect the relative lack of interest among our people in politics? The Hindu or indigenous performance in actual politics has also not been praiseworthy except for the three stars in an otherwise barren firmament. They were Maharana Pratap, Chhatrapati Shivaji and Maharaja Ranjit Singh. That is, therefore, a good reason for Indians to be alert about the goings-on in the country's political life. As one precaution, the writer suggests that voting in elections be made compulsory as it is in several countries like Belgium and Australia.

Abuse of Secularism

SIR MARK TULLY, former Bureau Chief of BBC, New Delhi, in a recent article has expressed his anguish at the spirit of secularism being abused, if not murdered. On the pathway to Partition, Muhammad Ali Jinnah and seven of his League colleagues wanted the maximum number of Muslims to migrate to the new holy land, and similarly, wanted Hindus and Sikhs to come away to India. Dr BR Ambedkar had supported this idea in his 1941 book *Thoughts on Pakistan*. Dr Rajendra Prasad, in his book *India Divided* had suggested that those Muslims who were unable to move should be allowed to reside in India on visas issued by New Delhi. Karachi was to look after similar arrangements for the Hindus and Sikhs there.

What should have been a straightforward arrangement was distorted by Gandhi's idiosyncrasies and Jawaharlal Nehru's political compulsions. He had become the leader of the Congress Parliamentary Party with virtually no support. The Muslims who remained behind in India were bewildered as to their future. Prime Minister Nehru used all the authority at his disposal to assure the non-migrant Muslims that they were safe. It is alleged that he went to the extent of rushing out on the streets of Delhi to protect their lives. He instructed the High Commissioner to Pakistan Sri Prakasa, to persuade those who had already migrated to return.

Nehru exhorted Bidhan Chandra Roy, then West Bengal's chief minister, to prevent persecuted Hindu refugees from East Bengal from crossing over to safety in India. There are letters from Nehru to Roy confirming these instructions. The Sikh leader, Master Tara Singh, proved too firm for Nehru and the latter was forced to let refugees from Punjab flow in. The Prime Minister showed his bias when he included Articles 25-30 in the Constitution giving special privileges to the minorities, a euphemism for the Muslims. These Articles were originally drafted not to please the Muslims, but to persuade the League to not insist on Partition. After the Partition, they had no relevance and, over the years, made the Hindus less than equal citizens.

An accurate definition of secularism was provided by Prof Bernard Stasi, who was commissioned by President Jacques Chirac of France. Stasi highlighted the three essential principles of secularism as: (a) religion and the individual; (b) the state and the individual, and; (c) the state and religion. The state is excluded from the relationship of (a). In the second (b), the state views the individual as a citizen and not as a member of a religious group. The implication of the third (c) is that religion and state function in two separate areas of human activity. The integrity of (a) and (b) is largely determined by the third relationship which separates them. Therefore, for any state to function as a secular state, it is of the utmost importance that there is a wall of separation between the State and the religion.

The state, however, has to maintain absolute neutrality between one religion and another. The French insistence on secularism or the absolute separation of the Church from the State goes back to 1905, when in December that year, a Republican Law was passed by the country's National Assembly. Its Article 1 assures the liberty of conscience. It guaranteed the free exercise of religious beliefs. The only restrictions were decreed in the interest of public order.

The Stasi Report emphasises secularism as a cornerstone of a democracy. Every state is sovereign and has the right to frame its Constitution as well as its other laws according to the needs of its society. How else has Malaysia declared itself an Islamic Republic, completely overlooking the presence of Hindus, Buddhists and Christians who comprise nearly half of the population? Why should Bangladesh and Pakistan have the privilege to call themselves Islamic? Bangladesh had reduced its Hindu population to 10 per cent by 1991. The figure for 2020 is not yet readily available. In 1947, Hindus comprised 30 per cent of East Bengal. Pakistan has today, according to its own census figures, only one and a half per cent Hindus. The rest have suffered ethnic cleansing. The fact that India has never challenged the rights of Bangladesh or Pakistan to do what they have done to their non-Muslim minorities means that we have respected their sovereignty. Moving further, would the Emirates in West Asia be justified in not allowing a temple to be built on their territory? Should Saudi Arabia have the right to disallow even the entry of a non-Muslim on the soil of Mecca and Medina? Does any universal declaration of human rights apply to these respected members of the international community in general and the UNO in particular?

In India, the practice during British rule was non-interference by the government in affairs of religion. This was especially so after the so-called Sepoy Mutiny of 1857. It was only after Independence and the advent of vote bank politics that *Sarva Dharma Sambhava* (equal respect for all religions) began to be twisted in order to play one community against the other. Articles 25 to 30 were first introduced in 1946 with the intention of dissuading the Muslim League from insisting on Partition. Mysteriously, however, they survived in the draft Constitution even after the country was torn asunder by Partition.

The Marxists also call themselves secular. Their idea, however, is active hostility against religion and religious symbols and practices. Karl Marx had considered religion to be the opium of the masses. In pursuance of this philosophy the Stalinists converted many a church, mosque and synagogue into shops, museums or offices, across the Soviet Union.

No doubt the Bible had laid the foundations of secularism—Matthew 22:21, in which Christ is quoted as saying: "Render therefore unto Caesar the things which are Caesar's; and unto God the things that are God's."

Hinduism has never been a structured religion, unlike Christianity. The concept of secularism, therefore, does not apply to this country. Tolerance is of utmost importance to Hindus. Even Jawaharlal Nehru did not think it fit to mention secularism as part of the Preamble of the Constitution. Indira Gandhi, under pressures of the Emergency, slipped this provision into it in 1976, at a time when her regime had thrown most opposition leaders behind bars and shackled democracy itself.

Nehru had cultivated the minorities for his support base. His successors used the same people as a vote bank in every election. They were believed to vote up to 90 per cent of their presence in the voters' list, whereas the others did not poll more than 35 to 40 per cent. This pampering of the minorities went to the extent of former Prime Minister Manmohan Singh repeatedly declaring that Muslims ought to have first claim on the country's resources.

Ayodhya to Sabarimala

THE CONTROVERSY OVER who can or cannot worship at the famous temple of Lord Ayyapan is unfortunate. That the apex court judges could not agree gave the impression that the differences may be unresolvable. There is a fear attached to it because this deity is the offspring of both Shankar and Vishnu, the latter in the version of the most ravishing beauty, Mohini. Mythology can be fascinating but also punishing when taken seriously. With the progress of time, certainly knotty corners should be unwound with acceptable common sense. A way has to be found without upsetting the sentiments of believing men and the faithful priests; upsetting worshipful women folk as well as not allowing a principle of justice to be violated. Say, throw open the temple to all men and women of all ages and leave it to the integrity and conscience of women to avoid the temple during their periods.

Similarly, one could think of ways and means of amicably settling the Ramjanmabhoomi issue at Ayodhya. There were several fundaments involved in the controversy but these were ignored. Most Hindus solemnly believed that Lord Rama was born on the spot where the Babri edifice existed. The universally popular epic *Ramayana* confirms that. If that was not sufficient, Poet Allama Iqbal called Lord Rama *Imam-e-Hind*. The Sunni Personal Law Board, however, would not give in; it wanted an apex court judgement to satisfy the Muslim *awaam* that it did not take the law into its own hands—that is in case it gracefully gave up its rights. It did not use its discretion lest its members be alleged to have compromised for any reason. Otherwise, the members displayed a lack of a sense of proportion. Where was the comparison between Hindu reverence for Lord Rama and Mir Baqi's edifice, possibly a maqbara? A masjid has at least one minaret for the muezzin to call followers to prayer especially in times when there were no microphones. There was no *woozu* for the followers to wash their hands and feet before offering namaz.

Yet another hesitation to giving up the spot to the Hindus could be the remaining temples, perhaps 3,000 in number, which were converted into mosques, a fact which is backed by evidence of records or epigraphs. Supposing the Hindus followed up Ayodhya with demands of more mosques and the land upon which they stand. If so, was this not unreasonable? How would Ayodhya and Rama's birthplace changing hands influence the other places? If at all, what could help the Muslims was goodwill and friendship which Ayodhya had a considerable scope for generating. In this regard, the Hindus did not help through the last many centuries. Their posture across the subcontinent has been so docile and defensive that Hindu goodwill was necessary or at least useful.

Going back to Sabarimala, the issue is one of the relationship of women with the divine. As a Hindu, the writer believes that no human would deceive the divine or even attempt such an unscrupulous adventure. The Hindu has faith in karma and its resulting fate. In the nature of this concept, each karma of each Hindu is self-recording. Even the most modern computer needs someone to make an entry by pressing a key. For the Hindu and his God there is nothing in between. The writer, therefore, cannot see a Hindu trying to deliberately deceive or even mislead the divine. A member of an Abrahamic religion like Judaism, Christianity and Islam may also sin but not try to deceive his/her God. What his/her God decrees or desires, the Christian follower can know by referring to the Bible which is the Christian scripture. What is outside the Bible is not his overriding concern.

Then there is the infidel who distinctly is deserving of a lower status. Coming to the Jew, the outer horizon of his morality extends to the *Torah* or whatever Prophet Moses said or wrote. The gentile is the Jew's version of an infidel. For the Muslim, the *kafir* is the infidel, with the Quran, the Hadith and the Sunnah being the ultimate guides. In contrast, the Hindu has no books that we can compare with, nor is he on par with an infidel or *kafir*. As a result, his/her conscience is the ultimate guide to moral action.

There is meant to be considerable, if not indefinite time lag, between his death and the doomsday and only one Almighty to sit in judgement on the performance of all his followers. The clergy may prescribe one or more means of atonement for a possible sin but, in his heart of hearts, the follower is afraid that he has sinned and may or may not be forgiven by God. For the Hindu lady at Sabarimala, what is the incentive to break the trust that she has been granted by the court and the temple, as suggested above? Why should a lady during her period venture into the temple?

Do the judges understand the nature and character of Indians? Until the demonetization of 2016, it was estimated that 40 per cent of the Indian economy was black which deprived the government of tax. Many a transaction was conducted either partly in white and partly in black or all black. Property dealings especially saw the give and take of cash as widely reported. But seldom has one heard of anyone being short-changed on the cash—promised one lakh and paid 75,000 rupees. Is that not integrity and faith? At the same time, there are numerous reports of banks suffering from NPAs and failure of repayment by borrowers. Does this mean that Indians are honest in private and opportunistic in public?

We must remember that this sought-after temple has its roots in the epic of the Ramayana. Lord Rama was in frantic search of his wife Sita who had been abducted by the Lankan ruler Ravana in the garb of a hermit. In the course of his search, Rama came across Shabri who had been waiting to have his *darshan* for a long time. Her guru *rishi*, before taking s*amadhi*, had told her that she must wait, as sooner or later, an avatar of Bhagwan Vishnu would be passing that way, and would bestow her with His *darshan*. Her *bhakti* for Rama was unfailing as proved by her collecting berries and tasting them before presenting them to Rama. Rama instantaneously reciprocated her faith. Similarly, the priests of the Sabarimala temple can display blind faith in the men worshippers who come. They do so after 40 days of abstinence from love, alcohol and shaving their beards. The first two of these continences for 40 days are readily accepted on faith. If the men can be trusted, why not the women is the question?

Standoff at the LAC

THE FIRST REQUIREMENT of any war is to assess the intention of the enemy. India learnt its lesson vis-à-vis China in 1962 with Jawaharlal Nehru as the Prime Minister and Krishna Menon as Defence Minister and advisor. On 20 August 1962, while boarding a flight to Colombo, Nehru told the media, "I have asked our troops to throw the Chinese out of our borders". Exactly two months later, on 20 October the enemy came hurtling down the North East Frontier (NEFA) hills, which are now known as Arunachal Pradesh. In the third week of November, Nehru wrote off the NEFA as well as Assam. The writer heard him say on the radio, "My heart goes out to the people of Assam (*Assam khatre mein hai*)", in which he included NEFA. A couple of days earlier, the State Bank had been ordered to empty its treasury in Tezpur, causing a scramble on the streets among the poor and the needy.

On the midnight of 20 November 1962, the Chinese army declared a unilateral withdrawal. In the colder regions, when a serious invader begins an invasion, it is generally in spring so that he has time enough to capture territory, then consolidate and decide on what he wants to do for the winter. The NEFA invasion commenced at 16,000 feet in autumn, where there was only ice in sight and no earth. Any additional Indian troops who needed to come up the mountains would be dressed in a single pullover, cotton uniforms and canvas shoes. Our army had no howitzers or standard mountain guns that could fire from peak to peak. Our soldiers had the WWII .303 bolt action rifles. Incidentally, the Chinese soldiers seen by our men had automatic rifles. The overwhelming logic for the Indian troops was to withdraw to the plains of Assam and to meet the enemy somewhat on a level playing field. But the generals we deployed in NEFA were evidently not competent. Neither Nehru nor Menon had any conception of war leadership.

We have come a long way since those dark days of Chinese humiliation. This time, the enemy action in Ladakh appears to be a message of objection to our reporting the weather in Muzaffarabad, Gilgit and Baltistan which are situated in Pakistan Occupied Kashmir (PoK). This was interpreted as a threat for the takeover of PoK. If we were to implement this action, China could lose quite a large portion of their prime One Belt One Road (OBOR), which is Beijing's dream project. In law, they are building this partly in our territory and they know it. They cannot afford to lose any part of this road. Nor can they risk an all-out war. A leading US Congressman Eliot Engels, also the Head of the House Committee on Foreign Affairs has somewhat raised the ante by voicing concern at

Chinese behaviour along the Line of Actual Control (LAC) at Ladakh. On the other hand, India has lost enough in Aksai Chin and there is certainly no scope for giving up any more territory, although during the debate on Aksai Chin Nehru had said on the floor of Parliament, "not a blade of grass grows there", to which Mahavir Tyagi, also a Congress MP, pointing to his bald head had retorted whether he too should treat it as useless. This retort reflected the anger of the parliamentarians.

China is on the horns of a dilemma. Can it afford to risk losing the sovereignty over a part of its proud belt and road project? That would not be the end of the saga of sovereignty. At stake would be Hong Kong, Tibet and Xinjiang, the Muslim province to its west which Mao Zedong captured rather curiously in 1950; it was formerly known as East Turkestan. Mao invited the Uyghur leaders to Peking (now Beijing). Most leaders of that rural province were tempted, especially when Peking offered to send them a chartered plane to come and go back. The political elite of East Turkestan, except for two communist leaders went to Peking, enjoyed themselves thoroughly and signed a treaty of friendship. The same aircraft carried them back. Unfortunately, the plane crashed on its return flight. There was no one left but the two communist leaders to takeover power in Urumqi, the capital of Xinjiang, which they did. Thereafter, the communists faithfully merged East Turkestan into China.

The stakes of the current dilemma are big. For some reason, many countries of the world seem to implicitly blame Wuhan for having delivered the Coronavirus or Covid-19 as it is popularly known, to the world. US President Donald Trump had said so openly, while other nations seem less eager to venture to openly blame China. This second-largest economy has a reverse problem of having to market most of its manufactured goods overseas. The question, therefore, is: where will the Chinese dilemma end? As far as India is concerned, we should be satisfied if a portion of our territory in Aksai Chin is returned. Similarly, Beijing should stop claiming sovereignty over Arunachal Pradesh.

But China has a great deal on its plate. In this day and age, its President Xi Jinping has declared himself emperor for life. Most senior members of the Chinese Communist Party (CCP) have been brought up on orthodox communist lines. To them, anything imperial, or for life, is an anathema. The apparent revolt in Hong Kong is an external symbol of resentment of imperialism. As a similar reaction, Taiwan has elected a nationalist president Tsai Ing-wen, who believes in a strong and stable relationship between her country and the USA.

With Barack Obama as president, the USA in no way felt threatened; China was looked upon as a supplier of cheap goods and depositor of good money. Donald Trump, being from a business background, detected that Xi Jinping's ambition was to replace the USA as the world's number one power. Various other suspicions have proliferated, such as China having launched a world war through Covid-19 that is currently ravaging the world. China and the US have locked horns over Coronavirus pandemic with Washington demanding a thorough investigation of the origin of the deadly virus which has claimed the lives of lakhs of people so far.

In the bargain, there is greater anti-China feeling than ever before. Amid on-going tension between the USA and China, American lawmaker Scott Perry introduced a bill in the Congress to authorise the than President Donald Trump to recognise Tibet as an independent nation. The same Republican has also introduced a similar bill for Hong Kong and these two bills have been referred to the House Committee on Foreign Affairs. This comes after Washington decided to revoke Hong Kong's special status, an act that Beijing was quick to dub as "most barbaric".

At one stage, nearly eight to ten years ago, the Chinese economy appeared to be racing ahead in its march to help the country achieve its dream of conquering the world. But all good and easy things do come to a halt. Workers are no longer prepared to work with compulsory low wages. There were three cheap factors in the cost of production, namely labour, land and loans. The latter two have stayed but the workers have raised their expectations. For several years, foreign investors have been whispering about their desire to move out of China. Some have moved to Vietnam and several other countries. But the real moving out has accelerated now, i.e., after the Hong Kong agitation.

The point being made is that the Chinese leaders have been fired by vaulting ambition. An English poet did advise his readers: "Let not thy ambition mock thy useful toil". Few readers, however, take the advice seriously and, therefore, their stakes in life are bound to be high. This is the way India should read the Chinese message of Ladakh.

Contentious Places of Worship

IS THE CURRENT time one of iconoclasm? Tayyip Erdoğan, the President of Turkey inaugurated the occasion by converting the Hagia Sofia Museum of Istanbul into a mosque on Friday, 24 July 2020. The building began life several centuries ago as a Greek pagan cathedral. It then became the grand temple of the Byzantine Greeks until they lost Constantinople to the invading Turks in 1453 AD. Sultan Mehmet converted it into a mosque. In 1931, the maker of modern Turkey, Kamal Mustafa Atatürk, secularised it into being a museum. Now again it has become a mosque.

Pakistanis have got inspired to convert Gurdwara Shahidi Asthan, built many years ago to commemorate the martyrdom of Bhai Taru Singhji at Naulakha Bazar in Lahore, into a mosque. India has protested and objected to such an act of desecration which would upset all the Sikhs here and spread panic to the community in that country. Bangladesh has not been quiet and on the fringes of Dhaka, some Hindu temples have been very recently destroyed. On 5 August 2020, the foundation stone of the new grand temple for Ram Lalla at Ayodhya was legitimately laid. The other three are illegitimate, iconoclastic actions.

We Indians have been under the impression that the Turks were keen to join the European Union (EU). Surely iconoclastic activity is not the way to win the Christian hearts over. In any case, many Muslims in Europe including up to five per cent of Germans are Turks. On the other hand, making a *masjid* through conversion does not especially impress Muslims if Erdoğan is chasing their votes. Moreover, Turkey is a member of the NATO and Donald Trump was no particular admirer of Islam.

The Pakistanis as well as Bangladeshis very well know that there are proven (documentary evidence or epigraphs) cases of over 3,000 temple desecrations and conversions into mosques across India. Systematic conversions from temples to mosques began on the morrow of the defeat of Prithviraj Chauhan at the Second Battle of Tarain in 1192 AD by Shahabuddin Ghori. When passing through Ajmer, he was impressed by a complex of three adjoining temples. He asked his slave assistant Qutbuddin Aibak to join them and convert them into a mosque within three days. Aibak achieved the task within sixty hours and therefore it has been called "*Adhai Din Ka Jhopda*". Ghori prayed here on his return journey. Incidentally, it is not too far away from the *dargah* of Moinuddin Chishti.

Chishti's *dargah* is also built on the remains of a demolished temple. In 1930s the Punjab High Court rejected the appeal of Lahore Muslims that the Sikhs should vacate the Shaheed Ganj Gurdwara (Shahidi Asthan) so the former could perform *namaz* as they did until the time of Maharaja Ranjit Singh. The Muslim League incited the Muslim legislators to go in further appeal to the Privy Council. The Punjab Premier Sir Sikandar Hayat Khan openly advised against such a pursuit on the ground that the Hindus could retaliate on a number of temples converted into mosques over the centuries. Sir Sikandar quoted Ajmer Sharif as an example and eventually no further appeal was made. In July 2020, Pakistanis took the law into their lands and converted the same gurdwara into a masjid.

It is the Muslims who invaded India, and demolished Hindu temples by the thousands. In 1992, 464 years later. the illegitimate replacement for the Ram Lalla mandir was brought down. After conceding Pakistan and not insisting that Muslims migrate, the Indian Muslims should have had the grace to offer the Babri structure on a platter to the Hindus. They know what Rama means to the Hindus. The Shias were so much more considerate than the Sunnis; their leader Ali Muhammad Jafar Rizvi withdrew all claims to the Babri structure.

The Muslims had been the conquerors since 1206 and had enjoyed Indian hospitality for these centuries. Obviously, there is no clash of interests between the communities but as Prof Samuel P Huntington had lucidly predicted there would be a fault line clash of civilizations. In his article *The Clash of Civilizations* (1993) he wrote:

> Fault line conflicts are communal conflicts between states or groups from different civilizations. Fault line wars are conflicts that have become violent. Such wars may occur between states, between nongovernmental groups, or between states and nongovernmental groups. Fault line conflicts within states may involve groups which are predominantly located in geographically distinct areas, in which case the group

> which does not control the government normally fights for independence and may or may not be willing to settle for something less than that. Within state, fault line conflicts may also involve groups which are geographically intermixed, in which case continually tense relations erupt into violence from time to time, as with Hindus and Muslims in India and Muslims and Chinese in Malaysia, or full-scale fighting may occur, particularly when new states and their boundaries are being determined, and produce brutal efforts to separate people by force.
>
> Fault line conflicts sometimes are struggles for control over people. More frequently the issue is control of territory. The goal of at least one of the participants is to conquer territory and free it of other people by expelling them, killing them, or doing both, that is, by "ethnic cleansing". These conflicts tend to be violent and ugly, with both sides engaging in massacres, terrorism, rape, and torture. The territory at stake often is for one or both sides a highly charged symbol of their history and identity, sacred land to which they have an inviolable right.

Incidentally, Sir Arnold Toynbee had visited Delhi and Bombay in 1961 to deliver the Azad Memorial Lectures. This was at the personal invitation of Jawaharlal Nehru. During the course of his lectures, Sir Arnold expressed surprise at having seen a mosque with tall minarets still standing on the banks of the river Ganga, the holiest of the holy places of the Hindus. This is despite India's independence. He went on to say that on his recent visit to Warsaw in Poland, he saw the cathedral in that city as a Roman Catholic edifice. When the Russians had conquered Warsaw a century or more ago, they had converted the earlier Catholic cathedral into a Russian orthodox church. The Poles could not tolerate this but were helpless. When they regained independence towards the end of World War I, they demolished the Russian church and rebuilt their own.

The Congress

THE CONGRESS SHOULD not be measured in terms of a typical political party like the Communist Party (Marxist), the Bharatiya Janata Party or the Hindu Mahasabha. These have distinct ideologies; they aim to remake India in the image of their respective ideologies. Anyone who is admitted as a member is expected to believe in their particular ideology. There are rules and procedures that each party tries to follow. The Congress, on paper, has all these, but in practice, operates on the "Führerprinzip" or the leadership principle. This was demonstrated vividly from 1977-79. Many a Congress stalwart tended to discount Indira Gandhi after she lost the 1977 election. For a few months, she had to lie low as a member of the Congress (K). The 'K' stood for K Brahmananda Reddy.

As the year progressed, the lady began to assert that she

ought to be the president of the party. Initially, the party stalwarts, many of whom still wore the white Gandhi cap and *khadi* attire, took no serious notice. Eventually, however, an AICC meeting was held on 31 December 1977. Well before midnight, Indira Gandhi left the meeting in a huff after informing the attendees that she would be available at the Glass House, which was one of the focal points of Bangalore. Soon after midnight, four Congressmen—Kamalapati Tripathi (UP), Subroto Mukherjee (West Bengal) and two others went to the Glass House. Led by Indira Gandhi as president, the Congress (I) came into being. It did not take many months for this party to proliferate in the then prevailing political scenario. Long before 1980, most Congressmen had shifted to the Congress (I). The Congress (K) disappeared and in its place, a dozen-member Congress (S) came into being, the (S) standing for socialist.

The media had rightly commented in those momentous months that the 'Congress is not where leaders attend. The Congress is where its supreme leader sits'. The then president of the Congress, Dev Kanta Barooah declared that "India is Indira and Indira is India" in 1974. In the 1980-81 general elections, the Congress (I) led by Indira Gandhi won a thumping victory and, thereafter, she ruled India till her assassination in October 1984. For those who are not entirely convinced by this theory of the Führerprinzip, they are entitled to other examples. In essence it is inner-party autocracy and not inner-party democracy that Vladimir Lenin had desired for the Bolshevik Party following the Russian Revolution of 1917.

Let us turn to Gandhi who practically ruled the Congress from 1920 to 1946. Netaji Subhas Chandra Bose won the Congress presidential election with a substantial majority in the

AICC, defeating Gandhi's favourite, Pattabhi Sitaramayya. The great leader strongly disapproved of Netaji's conduct. He had been president in 1938 and his standing again for the election was not to Gandhi's liking. He, therefore, saw to it that Netaji could not function in office. He ensured that the 21-member Congress Working Committee (CWC), comparable to the cabinet of a government, could not be formed. No one would join in the face of the displeased Bapu. Netaji Subhas was left with no choice but to leave the Congress Party; he resigned his presidentship and soon quit the Congress.

We now come to Jawaharlal Nehru who was a favourite of Gandhi but not of the Congress Party. In 1946, when its leaders were released from jail after the Quit India agitation, they realised that Maulana Abul Kalam Azad had been the party president for six years. It was time there was a change especially because Independence was in the air and whoever was Congress president was likely to become prime minister. As was the party procedure all the 16 Pradesh Congress Committees were consulted. Fifteen of the PCCs were for Sardar Vallabhbhai Patel and only one for Acharya Kripalani; no one showed any interest in Nehru. Yet Gandhi asked the Sardar to step aside and let Nehru become Congress president.

Thus Jawaharlal become president and then vice-president of the Interim government headed by Viceroy Mountbatten and partnered by the Muslim League. On 3 June 1947, the Viceroy declared Partition effective on 14 and 15 August and Nehru became prime minister of India. As an obedient disciple of Gandhiji, the Sardar worked earnestly as deputy prime minister and helped the government of India. Nehru came to be recognised as the leader of the party also and remained so until he died in May 1964. Notwithstanding the terrible failure of his China policy, the humiliation, and above all, the loss of territory by November 1962, Nehru remained prime minister and head of the Congress until he died. This shows to what lengths Congressmen were willing to go to remain loyal to their leader. To reiterate, out of loyalty to Gandhi, the party accepted Nehru, and out of loyalty to Nehru, they continued to support him no matter how great his blunders.

Indira Gandhi's main qualification was that she was Nehru's daughter. She was chosen as prime minister out of loyalty to her father. The handling of Sant Bhindranwale, the Akal Takht and the Punjab problem of 1984 left much to be desired. Yet, Congressmen remained loyal to their leader. They also accepted her son Rajiv Gandhi as the new general secretary of the party as if he was inevitably going to be their next leader.

After Indira Gandhi was assassinated, Congressmen patiently waited till Rajiv Gandhi was able to return to Delhi from West Bengal where he was on tour. He was ready to be sworn in as the next leader, when it was realised that the President was overseas. Giani Zail Singh was rushed to Rashtrapati Bhavan within minutes of having landed at Palam airport. He swore in Rajiv at exactly 6 pm, seven hours after BBC Radio had announced Indira's demise. As a loyal Congressman, Giani Zail Singh did not insist on Rajiv being elected leader of the parliamentary party. Till Rajiv was unfortunately assassinated at Sriperumbudur in 1991, no one questioned his presidentship of the party, although as prime minister he had lost the 1989 election. The bereaved family chose PV Narasimha Rao to be the successor. Despite being over 50 Lok Sabha votes short after the general election, Congressmen remained loyal to the government and Rao remained prime minister for his entire term.

Within days of Narasimha Rao being sworn in as prime

minister, he overturned the socialism planted by Nehru at the Congress's Avadi session in 1955. In less than two years, doubts were cast that Rao also overturned secularism, which had been fathered by no less than Gandhi. The Muslims widely believe that the Rao Government had a hand in the demolition of the Babri edifice at Ayodhya. Yet, he remained PM till the end of his term in 1996. Thereafter, the party was on the lookout for a more permanent leader. Sonia Gandhi was elected, defeating the only opposing candidate (late) Jitendra Prasada in November 2000. To this day, she remains president of the Congress.

Constitution

THE RE 1 fine imposed by the Supreme Court on 31 August 2020 on activist lawyer Prashant Bhushan for two tweets that the court found derogatory drew my attention to the foundation of our Constitution. The Preamble begins with justice, liberty, equality and fraternity from which presumably emerge socialist and secular. All very noble sentiments, but not at all rooted in the Indian ethos. To me, the moral cornerstone of Indians is *karma*. Those citizens who are immigrants into the country and have not yet adjusted to the soil may not be *au fait* with this but all others, including people of non-Hindu religions, know it. Karma is the root of life and is known to even illiterate Indians. The Indian Constitution should, therefore, be ideally rooted in karma and not liberty, equality and fraternity, the troika of words thrown up by the French Revolution of 1789.

Together the words sound resonant but those who speak or hear them do not realise that they are contradictory. Liberty or freedom is spontaneous and most people are born free; whereas equality is not natural and has to be imposed by society or government. Almost everyone is born unequal. Excellence has to be reduced and ordinariness has to be supported to bring about equality or near-equality. Many a person has to be supported to bring about equality. The moment society loosens its grip, equality goes and liberty takes over. The essence of karma is liberty and is utterly rational and logical. In life, the consequence of karma is *bhagya* or fate; the deed leads to destiny. This is rather like the principle of physics that for every action there is an equal and opposite reaction.

Equality is an Abrahamic innovation; the first Prophet and his successors believed that God made man equal but society makes him unequal. The result is that every good Christian believes in the desirability of social service, whether by running schools, colleges or hospitals. Islam introduced *zakat*, a kind of tax of two and a half per cent of every faithful follower's wealth at the end of every year. The money so raised is used by the holy men for the welfare of poor Muslims. These are the ways Christians and Muslims try to make people as equal as possible. The sentiments are noble, but to what extent do they succeed in bringing about equality? The faith in karma believes that a person is poor or suffering as a result of his deeds, past or present, good or bad. Or he or she is well-off and happy as a reward for desirable deeds done earlier. Charity cannot be an equaliser of the essentially unequal. Nor can karma be controlled down or up. No society has been able to achieve equality, including the former Soviet Union which was based on the ideology of Marxism, which proclaimed "from each according to his ability to each according to his need". The intentions of Karl Marx and Vladimir Lenin remained on paper but the Soviet Union certainly went bankrupt in a matter of seventy years.

Karma, as the root of life, is at least as old as the *Vedas* if not older. On the other hand, the inspiration to socialism may be vaguely traced to Plato's *Republic* or Greek philosophy. The second written inspiration was Thomas More's *Utopia*, a title which is self-explanatory of socialism's deficiency in realism. In any case, it has no connection with the Indian ethos. Incidentally, when the Constitution was first inaugurated in 1950, there was no mention of socialism. It was smuggled into the Preamble in 1976 (Emergency year) when most opposition leaders were in jail. However, Jawaharlal Nehru in 1956 had introduced his economic policy as a socialistic pattern of society.

Secularism was similarly smuggled into the Preamble of the Constitution in 1976. It had no meaning for India, a dominant Hindu country with no religion ruling in government. Hinduism is not a religion in the sense of one way of worship, one God, one holy book, one prophet. Its core is karma and thereafter there are innumerable denominations. Strangely enough, secularism began as a revolt against the Roman Church seen by many a German as practicing imperialism. For example, three lakh pieces of gold used to be taken annually from the German speaking areas by Rome with no benefit to the Germans. Martin Luther led the protest which eventually resulted in the Reformation in the 16th century. France largely remained loyal to Rome and there were three houses in its Parliament or National Assembly—House of the landed aristocracy, House of Commons and thirdly the House of bishops and abbots. The Church owned a great deal of land and had a substantial voice in governance. The king listened more to the Church and the others probably kept quiet for fear of God. When the French Revolution took place, the country still had the three houses. In the light of these facts one can see why secularism or the separation of the State from the Church took place. What was the relevance of these developments to India?

While Dr BR Ambedkar drafted the Constitution, it was Jawaharlal Nehru who directed it to the end. For the sake of communal peace, Articles 25 to 30 were introduced. The first, namely 25, gives freedom of conscience and free practice and propagation of religion. It gives complete freedom to change one's religion.

Article 27 gives freedom regarding payment of taxes for the promotion of any particular religion so long as non-payers are not coerced. Article 28 allows freedom for attendance at religions instruction or religious worship in certain educational institutions. With all these provisions, there is no justification for Hindus to complain that any of these provisions leads to minority pampering.

The Christians regularly propagate the faith of Christ. They also teach this message in their schools. Muslims raise a tax called *zakat* for distribution to the poor who need not be of their faith. The Hindus do not do any such thing except to keep announcing *ghar wapsi* (back to home)—a series of conversion activities by Hindu organisations to facilitate conversion of Christians and Muslims to Hinduism. Whether the Constitution should have been so liberal as to allow conversion, which would be the result of propagation, is a matter of opinion.

Article 41 provides the right to work, to education and to public assistance for the purpose. The national document was first released on 26 January 1950, but after all these years, teaching poor children is not fully in gear.

To achieve cent per cent school education there should be a public and private collaboration. The State can provide the land and a prosperous industry should construct the building, after which public donations could be raised for other expenses like furniture, smart boards and other equipment. Token fees should be charged because anything that comes free is taken for granted both by the parents and children. If no restriction is placed, a period a day could be used for moral education, teaching moral values, including religious ones. More private parties could be attracted to participate in this grand collaboration for teaching India's children. In fact, it is useful for children to grow up knowing the fundaments of all faiths. There would then be little communal tension.

Muslims Deserve Empathy

IF ONE COMES into close and continuous contact with conscientious Muslims, however small in number, one would realise how paradoxical their situation is. For many Muslims the choice of remaining in India at the time of Partition was made by their grandparents. If one goes by how the non-Punjabi Muhajirs have been treated in Pakistan, the choice of staying back in India was visionary. Notwithstanding some fears expressed in 1947, the Muslims who stayed back were treated well by the Nehru government. As one of them told me, his father said that they never expected that they would be treated as welcome guests. They were given special rights, be it in their personal law or education, or in the matter of their worship. Madrasa schools and universities like Aligarh, or marriage and divorce laws were well-protected. The government reformed

Hindu laws but left Mohammedan law alone. Muslim leaders seldom bothered about how Hindus felt. The result was the 2014 general election.

As the sands of time proceeded, the Muslims began to experience Hindu resistance to cow slaughter, right or wrong, real or imaginary. Many Hindu liberals and secularists sympathised with the Muslims. Opposition politicians protested while the Muslims felt that their status had slipped. They were no longer guests in India as someone wisecracked. No one could predict the situation; most people presumed that the flame of Hindu politics was extinguished when Nathuram Godse gunned down Gandhi in 1948. In the meantime, conditions in Pakistan going downhill, many Muslims felt that regardless of everything, their grandparents' decision against migration and to stay back in India had been the correct one. Today, the question Muslims ask is: are we heading towards a second-class citizenship?

They are feeling insecure and troubled. Muslims do not realise that while some of their feelings might be justified, others are hallucinations. Why is it that the Christians who also worship an Abrahamic way do not share all these apprehensions? Nor does any other minority. Is it because Muslims have been brought up to believe that they are special citizens? Is it because they have an uneasy conscience about the Partition?

Whatever it be, one thing is certain—they feel that they are less educated and, therefore, more backward than the other communities in India. If this be so, its roots go back to the frowning upon *ijtehad* (reinterpretation) and insistence on *taqlid* (orthodoxy) for the last thousand years. The holy Quran is a direct revelation of Allah's message to Prophet Mohammad. It should, therefore, be followed faithfully and not be subjected to questioning. Permission to engage in *ijtehad* would sooner or later lead to debate, which could lead to loosening of the faith in Islam.

Prof Timur Kuran, a Turkish-born American who teaches at Duke University (USA) has a somewhat different opinion. His study shows that backwardness amongst Muslims is due to inhibitions placed upon the community by the theology. In his well-known book *The Long Divergence: How Islamic Law Held Back the Middle East*, he says: if asked to explain why the modern economy took shape in north-western Europe and not the eastern Mediterranean (where the Middle East begins), the typical answer would contrast Western flexibility with Muslim rigidity. The strict adherence to *taqlid* by the faith opposes any innovation. Islamic laws of the Middle East engendered social structures that resisted adaptation and advancement.

Outlining the economic picture of the Middle East, Prof Kuran makes clear the fact that until the late eighteenth century no major religious community of the Middle East outclassed others in either commerce or finance. However, as global economic modernisation progressed, Christians and Jews registered advances that Muslims failed to match. The former two communities leapt ahead of Muslims in living standards. Strict Islamic law on one hand made Muslims shun interest and look down on commerce. On the other hand, Western commercial networking became modernised with the march of progress. It became intertwined with institutions that facilitated impersonal exchanges, which made trade and commerce with Westerners more lucrative. Because of Islamic law, Muslims both failed to create such institutions or to derive any benefit from the Western institutions that existed.

What Prof Kuran has said does not apply to Indian Muslims

entirely. There are three sects in Gujarat who have enterprise running in their veins. They are the Khojas, who were the Lohanas of Kathiawad who were comparatively recently converted to Islam; Mohammad Ali Jinnah's father's name was Jinabhai, which is a Hindu name. The Qaid-e-Azam went to England with a passport with his Hindu surname and was registered at the Lincoln's Inn accordingly for his barristership.

The Kutchi Lohanas who happened to be converted became Memons who are Musalmans. The third sect is Bohras, who were originally Brahmins. They are those who believe in twelve *imams* unlike the Khojas or Aga Khanis, who put their faith in seven imams. All these three sects as a whole are as good traders as any *bania*. For the rest of the Muslims, the same compliment cannot be paid. To a large extent Muslims were ruling India when the British arrived. It was Mughal Emperor Jahangir who issued the first *firman* for the East India Company represented by Robert Clive to drive the nawabs of Bengal, Bihar and Orissa from the throne. The Battle of Plassey in 1757, and the history thereafter, are well-known. In 1799, Lord Wellesley defeated and killed Tipu Sultan at the Battle of Seringapatam. That ended the sultanate in South India. In 1856, Lord Dalhousie deposed Nawab Wajid Ali Shah and freed UP of Muslim rule.

A reaction to all this was the Sepoy Mutiny the following year. The British blamed the Muslims for this revolt. At the time the alleged culprits were being hanged near the Delhi Gate, up to ninety per cent of them were Muslim. Yet, leaders like Sir Syed Ahmed Khan, the founder of the Aligarh Muslim University, turned the Muslim sentiment against Hindus and called the '*Ahl-e-Kitab*' British their allies. Thereafter, Justice Ameer Ali, poet Allama Iqbal and of course, MA Jinnah, played on this separate nation theory and achieved Partition, notwithstanding a number of individuals and institutions like the university at Deoband opposing the bifurcation of the country. There is reason to believe, therefore, that the attention and energy of the Muslims was diverted away from their progress and yoked to politics.

On Modi

THE ENIGMA THAT is Prime Minister Narendra Modi is impossible to understand, unless of course one has the time, energy and imagination to do so. Looking at him as a politician, one would not find one similar, either now or in the past and one would be hard-pressed to escape confusion.

As is obvious to most people, Modi believes in worship and his faith in *paramatma* is total. Yet, he is by no means given to fatalism. Whatever will be will be, *que sera sera* is not for Modi. His dharma is that of a *karma yogi*. His *karmabhoomi* is the country. His love for the country is supreme; nothing else matters to him. In fact, he has no lasting attachment except to the country which is also his only love.

It is not customary to say thank you in Gujarat. As a result, Shri Modi does not acknowledge good work done with a formal thank you. His reasoning is: if I live and work for the country and you happen to help, what great obligation are you creating and for whom? The Rashtriya Swayamsevak Sangh encourages its *pracharaks* and *vistaraks* to make contacts and keep in touch with people. If any family invites one to lunch, it is a welcome sign; the person has been liked. This builds up a relationship. Reciprocation is not necessary or practical for a bachelor living in a hostel. Once at Savarkundla in Saurashtra, Gujarat, I happened to be invited for lunch by a party worker. The little gathering was enjoyable. At the end I happened to say thanks, as is the Delhi habit. The host's face fell, and I, being disturbed at the sight asked him why. His reply was, 'Your saying thanks means that when I come to Delhi I will feel there is no need for you to ask me to your home for a meal.' I felt sorry and embarrassed at what I had done. After all, I hail from that part of the country and should have known better.

On a bright morning in early 2001, we happened to be chatting briefly at the rear of the main building of the BJP office. I happened to mention to Narendrabhai that, in my opinion, it was high time he took the plunge into electoral politics, to which his reply was that he had to be told to do so by the Sangh but he could not ask for a ticket; that was the tradition. This statement drew my admiration to his sense of discipline as well as his restraint in respecting what was customary. When he did go to Gujarat to take over the chief ministership, it was on Advani's instructions.

It was evident even in those early days that Modi had enormous leadership potential. That, however, gave him no early advantage and his ride in politics was far from smooth. While his organisational capabilities and grasp of the nitty-gritty of political work was much in demand, his persona and spontaneous influence over the rank and file of the party was a niggling worry to the entrenched satrapy. Former chief minister of Gujarat Keshubhai Patel made good use of Modi, though, to keep his arch rival in state politics, Shankersinh Vaghela, down.

Once Vaghela had been eased out from the BJP, Narendra Modi ceased to be Keshubhai's favourite. Modi had outlived his utility for Patel. Keshubhai wasn't content with merely sidelining Modi; he had him transferred to Delhi as organising General Secretary of the BJP. This was no ordinary political transfer. Keshubhai had enforced a stipulation that if ever Modi visited his home state, he would not meet any politician or journalist and would confine himself only to personal matters. It was thus a veritable political *vanvaas* or exile for Modi. This was indeed a tough and unpleasant phase of Narendra Modi's political life.

When I happened to be in the BJP office at Ahmedabad a couple of weeks later, I was escorted by Anandiben Patel, currently Governor of Uttar Pradesh, Dr Mayaben Kondani and five other ladies. They protested about Narendrabhai's unfortunate situation and the grave injustice done to him in the form of exile from Gujarat. I conceded their point that Keshubhai's move was unjust, but asked them whether they considered Ramchandra, the avatar of Vishnu, to be great, to which they replied in the affirmative. My next question was: would Ram have been so great if he had not been sent on his *vanvaas* or exile to the forest? No, was their answer. I then told them that Narendrabhai was undergoing a similar *vanvaas*! When Modi became the chief minister of Gujarat at the end of 2001, Anandiben Patel affirmed that she hadn't forgotten my prediction about NaMo, as he was popularly known.

Overall, what was noteworthy was that he did not arrive in

Delhi when he knew that the Sangh Parivar was apprehensive of tensions in Congress. He stuck to discipline and did not come until he was asked to do so by the sarsanghchalak of the RSS, after it was decided at the *baithak* in Goa that Narendra Modi would lead the campaign for 2014 general elections. This was the implicit signal that he would be the prime-ministerial candidate. His ingrained discipline was demonstrated when he bowed his head to the ground before climbing the steps to the Parliament House. This was also his signal that he was not flattered by his victory, but that he was grateful to the Almighty at being given an opportunity to serve his first and only love, as its *pradhan sewak*. No wonder that he has ruled since for the sake of the country and its people and not for himself or his family. This is what Krishna taught in the course of the *Mahabharata*. He enabled the Pandavas and Yudhishthira to sit on the throne of Hastinapur, but never aspired to the throne himself, nor did he promote his own community for it.

This selfless dedication must have helped Modi to achieve not only national acclaim but international fame too. We cannot ignore the fact that no Indian leader before him has addressed the British Parliament. Nor has any leader ever been honoured by the British monarch by hosting an exclusive lunch for him.

Incidentally, the Prime Minister has also addressed the Australian Parliament as well as the US Congress, not to speak of the many world leaders he has made friends with. All this and more has helped India to attain heights unknown before.

Who Demolished the Babri Structure?

THERE ARE TWO persons who should be especially remembered by Ram devotees who hope to reach the seventh heaven when the new mandir at Ayodhya is completed. For, without them, the Supreme Court would not have been able to give any order nor could anyone have been able to build the new temple. Ram Lalla would have been left indefinitely under the roof of the Babri structure. The reason is simple—without these gentlemen's initiative it is unlikely that the Babri structure could have been brought down. Also built anywhere else in Ayodhya, it would not be a Ramjanmabhoomi temple.

The then future chief ministers of Gujarat, Keshubhai Patel and Sureshbhai Mehta were keen to be in Ayodhya on 6 December 1992. They asked me if I could take them since I was Delhi-based and had a large enough car. Frankly, I was also keen to go. We spent a night each at Bareilly and Lucknow. On the third day we reached Ayodhya at 10.30 in the morning. Being known VIPs, the three of us were conducted to the terrace earmarked for leaders. Whatever ground we could see from the first floor high terrace of Ayodhya, was all covered by people, local as well as from various corners of the country. We had to stay put there without any food, water or relief until 5.30 pm. When we came down from the terrace, it was cold and pitch dark and we could see two vehicles burning at a distance. Evidently some rioting was taking place. Sureshbhai's little radio told us that all four state governments ruled by the BJP had been dismissed. The Governors had taken over as central rulers.

We reached back Lucknow where there was a curfew by 9pm. A little later, Prime Minister Narasimha Rao was addressing the nation on the TV and the central thrust of his speech was condemnation of the reported demolition. He repeatedly promised the audience that his government would rebuild the masjid. My reaction was where was the need to rebuild? Only the domes had collapsed while all the walls were standing. At least that was the situation when we left the terrace at Ayodhya.

It is uncanny that I am yet to meet anyone who has seen a photograph of the structure with no domes and all walls standing. By the morning of 9 December, there were pictures in the newspapers of Ram Lalla *virajman* in a tent and not a sign of the erstwhile masjid, which meant that within sixty hours or so from our leaving Ayodhya, the entire structure had disappeared? What a colossal piece of work by whoever demolished such thick, tall walls with all the rubble of the fallen domes and all debris cleared.

As I went to bed, I was assailed by thoughts of what if the walls were brought down, rather than the domes being replaced? Indian history might change its course. Dr Ram Swarup, the distinguished Indologist had told me once when I went to call on him, that at least 3,000 such mosques had been identified in the country. Before I fell asleep, I had wondered what if the attention of the Vishwa Hindu Parishad had turned to some or all these temples turned mosques? At the laying of the foundation stone of the grand temple on 5 August 2020, the prime minister incidentally mentioned the possibility of more excitement in the future.

I realised that the day we had spent on the terrace was mysterious but I was too tired to unravel anything that night. For several days, however, I could not take my mind off the events as they had unfolded on the terrace. There was only one mike and Acharya Dharmendra was successfully keeping the crowd engaged if not also amused. Uma Bharati also helped a great deal with her eloquent speaking. Occasionally, leaders intervened to appeal to those who had climbed on to the domes to come down. I especially remember HV Sheshadri of the RSS and LK Advani speaking. No one appeared to know what would happen eventually. A little after 1 pm, two journalists came up to the terrace. They were very disturbed, almost ready to break down; their cameras had been hurled to the ground and they had visibly been beaten. There was blood on their faces; I was surprised because I had never before seen pressmen treated so badly. They had been near the first dome shooting the men who, with iron crowbars, were attacking the joints between the walls and the domes.

That was heavy-duty professional work. The men told the journalists not to use the cameras but five of them kept doing so. Usually, political workers welcome being photographed; evidently these men did not. The pressmen could not understand and turned a deaf ear to their request. Eventually they snatched the cameras and dashed them to the ground. In the scuffle to save their equipment, these gentlemen were quite badly hurt and felt humiliated. I was a sympathetic listener and came to know what exactly was happening and who these men at work were. They were evidently PWD professionals and were bringing down the domes.

Sure enough, at 2.30 pm, the right dome crashed; it needed the professionals to weaken the edge of a dome for it to come down. The excitement on the terrace could be imagined and, of course, the masses on the ground became delirious. After the photographers had gone, I turned to the lady police officer standing nearby. She was a senior IPS officer. I asked her why there was no police intervention; after all property was being damaged. Her reply was that the police had clear instructions not to interfere unless a human life was hurt or attacked.

When asked, she assured me that they had 15,000 Central Reserve Police at Faizabad, 4 km away. At about 3.30 pm a young priest rushed up to the terrace with a white woollen shawl, holding it as if he was protecting something inside. He was given a seat on the bench. He showed the two little black idols of Ram and Lakshman. He said he had saved them from getting crushed in the event the central dome fell. The senior *mahant* had permitted him to do so and to take the idols for the senior leaders on the terrace to see. Below, one could see dozens of young men carrying away souvenirs from the structure. At 3.40 pm another dome collapsed while the last went down at 4.30. Most leaders on the terrace celebrated with tears of joy at what they had seen while a few senior ones appeared sombre in their anxiety as to what would happen next. After 5 pm everyone began to move towards the narrow staircase.

The whole of 7 December and a part of the 8th were spent returning to Delhi. It was not until the 9th that I could fully reflect on the events of 6 December and imagine what must have happened thereafter at Ayodhya. On looking back two points became clear. At Ayodhya, there were only UP policemen. At Faizabad were the Central Reserve Police—neither to move unless there was violence on people. Similarly, there must have been in the surroundings, sufficient PWD force with bulldozers and what not. After night fall, they all must have gone to work systematically after the police persuaded the people to go home. Buses had been provided to take people to stations free of charge, as reported in the newspapers of those days.

All day, there was perfect coordination between the State and the Centre. After 5.45 pm on the 6th, there was no State government; only the Central government with the Governor in full command to deal with the structure first and then its debris. So that, in about sixty hours, the ground was clear for Ram Lalla to be established in the special tent.

Congress Bets Only on Charisma

MR YOGENDRA YADAV, current national president of Swaraj India, would like the Congress party to die for the sake of the country's political welfare, so that space is created for a new opposition organisation to come up to help remove the Modi regime. Evidently, Yadav is afflicted with anger; or else he would not make such an irrational statement. The Congress has an enormous brand equity which is essential for a party to get to anything like a national acceptability. India is not only very large but has many languages and different cultures. Within a language group too, there are differences; perhaps inherited from the caste system. Then there are variations in development; some are still at the cultural level of the nineteenth century while others are already on the cusp of the 22nd.

To get identified with such a wide variety of people is very difficult. For a new party to grow into a national formation, opposing the BJP and removing its leadership would not only be a Herculean challenge but might take decades upon decades to be successful. One may note that for all its successes, the BJP has not yet been able to reach out effectively to the people of Tamil Nadu, Kerala and Andhra Pradesh. Its prototype the Jana Sangh was founded in 1951, some 68 years ago. I doubt if there has come up a third alternative. A Delhi-based party is hopeful of going national. I wonder if Mr Yadav, when he was its member, had provided the inspiration?

The Congress has a unique record. It began with informing the British rulers how the Indian intelligentsia felt about their policies and actions. Gradually, it started agitating for freedom for Indians. In such a cause, virtually anyone was welcome to join, whether Indian or foreigner; the party's founder was an Englishman, Allan Octavian Hume. Until the advent of Mohandas Gandhi, the Congress was a gentlemen's set-up, rather like a club. It was in 1921, with the Non-Cooperation Movement that it began to take on the character of a mass party. Soon Gandhi became its leader and led it until Jawaharlal Nehru took over; after his death, his daughter Indira took over.

In October 1984, after being shot by her bodyguards, Mrs Gandhi had been declared dead by the doctors at AIIMS hospital and the tragic news was broadcast by the BBC radio by 11 am. But Akashvani and Doordarshan kept this development under wraps until 6 pm, by when President Zail Singh had returned to India and was ready to swear in Rajiv Gandhi as prime minister. This subterfuge showed how important leadership was to the Congress. By then the party had hardly any assets except its brand equity. Until 1969, the Congress had virtually everything that a political party might want. But with its split in 1969, the assets, including the organisational network, remained with the Congress O (Organization). Mrs Gandhi's Congress R (Requisition) had nothing except the members who were personally loyal to her. As it happened, she chose not to have assets. Several Pradesh Congress Committees operated from their president's residence. For instance, Ajit Panja of West Bengal used the drawing room of his residence at 250, Chittaranjan Avenue, Kolkata. Many a member wedded to tradition would swear not to go to his house. Mrs Gandhi must have received complaints but she did not care. Evidently, she did not trust many. By 1980, half the District Congress Committees did not exist. She depended on her charisma and her mass following; the party members were powerless helpers in promoting her cause.

Many Congressmen by then had also come to believe that the Nehru-Gandhi family had a unique charisma amongst the Indian masses. They believed that Mohandas Gandhi had transformed the Congress into a mass party and it flourished under his charisma, until Jawaharlal Nehru took the baton from him. After Nehru, Indira Gandhi effectively played this role and enabled the Congress to dominate the Indian political scene. Thereafter, Rajiv Gandhi played a yeoman's role in keeping the party flying high. For the first and the only time, he led over 400 Congressmen in the Lok Sabha. If he lost the 1989 elections, it was because of Bofors more than anything else. In the 1990s, many Congressmen missed a Gandhi at the helm. They found it difficult to swallow the leadership of PV Narasimha Rao. Muslim members were heard whispering under their breath that it was he who destroyed the Babri Masjid. This is to illustrate the frustration among party members.

When Sitaram Kesari was party president, several rumour

mongers would say that their historic party would break up. Little wonder that the only Gandhi available, namely Mrs Sonia Gandhi, was elevated to the ivory throne of the Congress. The party members had no inhibitions, as it had been founded by an Englishman. It was later presided over by an Irishwoman, Annie Besant, and subsequently by Nellie Sengupta. For Congressmen, the priority was a charismatic Gandhi, no matter whether brown or white.

There is a fundamental reason for a charismatic leadership to keep the Congress together. That reason is that the party is primarily a platform of politicians to meet for the pursuit of power. Especially after Independence, it had no particular cause, nor an ideology to hold it together. Little wonder that Mohandas Gandhi recommended its dissolution post-independence. In the great man's own time, the Congress had opposed Partition but, without much hesitation had accepted the division after Jinnah's Direct Action Day, inaugurated by the Great Calcutta Killings of August 1946.

To quote a more recent example, the Congress had won the 1991 general election on a socialistic manifesto. Within a week, however, it gave a go-by to all socialism and liberalised the economy on the basis of an International Monetary Fund (IMF) prescription. This freedom from ideology has enabled the Congress to induct members from all walks of political life, whether an Akali like Sardar Zail Singh, a Communist like PR Kumaramangalam, or a Shiv Sainik like Chhagan Bhujbal, et al. The flip side of this convenience is the indispensability of charismatic leaders as binders or unifiers.

The political acumen that Mr Yogendra Yadav yearns for is not an essential component of charisma. Rajiv Gandhi did not have it. Be that as it may, what is necessary is for the party to find such a leader rather than wanting the Congress to die. In any case, the Congress is not a roadblock to the rise of a third national party. The pathways for the rise of such a party are innumerable in our large country.

Modi, the Faith Keeper

THE RETURN OF Mr Narendra Modi with a generous mandate for the second time makes it necessary to go into the rest of the phenomenon. When he was elected in 2014, there were experts who felt that the people had voted with their feet. Even tolerant Indians could not take the gargantuan corruption presided over by the personally honest Dr Manmohan Singh. Being entirely new to Delhi and central politics, Modi was looked upon as a parvenu, who would play out his time rather like a cricket nightwatchman. With demonetization, many a veteran of the Lutyens establishment was astounded. Actually, if an economy is to be modern, it cannot indefinitely run on two tracks, white and black: the latter had to be eventually eliminated. This did not make the veterans more sympathetic to Modi. Instead, in order to condemn demonetization, they innovated the expression "informal sector" for the black economy.

The General Sales Tax (GST) was originally initiated by the Manmohan Singh government, and yet, when the Modi government introduced it, the tax was repeatedly criticised by Manmohan's party, the Congress. Modi's Pakistan policy was frequently denounced until Balakot. That he was the first Indian leader to be invited to address the British Parliament, and to be invited for an exclusive lunch by Her Majesty the Queen at Buckingham Palace evoked no compliment from the honourable opposition. Instead, the Prime minister was accused of destroying institutions. In short, Mr Modi remained a parvenu in the Lutyens circle, which hoped he would be marginalised in the just-held general election. In order to make sure that he does not return to power, the Congress president called him a thief on an average three times a day. Unfortunately for the Congress president and his party, the people of India decided otherwise.

Why have the people of India chosen Mr Modi for a second term in the face of the most furious opposition that any prime ministerial candidate has ever faced in independent India? Every political party in opposition had one common agenda which was to remove Modi from power. Such a unanimous opposition agenda was last seen in 1977 against Indira Gandhi's Emergency. The masses of India have perceived Narendra Modi as the first leader who has risen from the soil and who loves his motherland more than anything else. The people who have faith in him have not been disappointed. He has ruled for the last five years for the people and the country and not for himself. No previous prime minister could be tested on this touchstone. I do not think that this faith and sentiment are confined only to the Hindus; it extends to quite a number of Christians, Muslims and others.

Narendra Modi has modernised the country. It is true that Jawaharlal Nehru was for his time a modern thinker. He did think of building irrigation dams, factories that could build advanced machines, starting Indian Institutes of Technology as well as Management, giant steel plants and so on. However, while Nehru did build numerous temples of modernity in a dominantly agrarian society, he did not bring about a revolution in the minds of the people that they needed to modernise. In other words, he could not convert modernisation into a mass movement.

Rajiv Gandhi was brought up in a contemporary environment and had spent time in England, and learnt to fly aircraft. He understood machines and chose the best passenger aircraft in the Airbus. An equally good choice was the Bofors artillery gun, if we overlook for a while the financial scandal attached to it. Gandhi grew up parallel with the growth of the computer and could operate the electronic machine with aplomb, and he did try to introduce its use in government institutions. But before he could go far, he lost the 1989 election and went out of power. In any case, he might not have been able to go very far because he could not motivate men with the same aptitude he could move machines. Before we move to another prime minister, we should not forget to record that millions of telephones were installed in India during Rajiv Gandhi's time.

Prime Minister PV Narasimha Rao, compelled by dire financial circumstances as he stepped into power, did bring about an economic revolution. From a party wedded to a socialistic pattern of society, it had now no choice but to overturn it into promoting *laissez faire* (abstention by government from interfering in the workings of the free market). In short, he embarked on a path of economic liberalisation as a step towards globalisation. Atal Bihari Vajpayee took liberalisation forward to some extent. His main contribution, however, was introducing the construction of modern highways, which can be considered a step towards modernisation.

To come back to Narendra Modi, he launched modernisation along with preaching its importance from the ramparts of the Red Fort in his first Independence Day speech. He began with the importance of cleanliness to society with the slogan Swachh *Bharat*. Even earlier, his election campaign theme of 2014 was development, which willy-nilly implied modernisation. "*Sabka Saath Sabka Vikas*" clearly implies participation of all for the purpose of progress.

One of the first steps Modi took after becoming prime minister was to abolish the Planning Commission with the help of a cabinet resolution. This was possible because Nehru had set up the Commission by a cabinet decision. Such a Herculean economic step was taken without going to Parliament, perhaps because Nehru was apprehensive that the comparatively conservative members of the Constituent Assembly might not approve of such a commission. After all, national planning was introduced by the Soviet Union in the name of Gosplan. Incidentally, one of the reasons for the collapse of the Soviet economy was the excessive powers assumed by Gosplan.

As the years went by, the Yojana Bhawan in Delhi began being misused for manipulating power over the states. Money was allotted generously, provided the state government toed the central government line. Whether the money allocated was used or misused depended on the state government. The Planning Commission's work ended with sanctioning the year's

Plan expenditure. The Finance Ministry disbursed the money. Thereafter, implementation and monitoring were entirely the state's function. In the bargain, there was over-expenditure, misuse of funds and inflation. With the abolition of the Commission, inflation has come down quite remarkably.

There are any number of reforms that were introduced especially keeping the poor people in mind. It is not that the previous governments had not thought of them, but a large chunk of the money earmarked was kept back by middlemen. As Rajiv Gandhi in his time had said, only 15 per cent reached the poor person. Mr Modi's policy has been to ensure that all poor people should have their own bank accounts, wherein monies due to them can be remitted directly. All in all, it would be fair to say that through the last millennium, India experienced popular *badshahs* and hateful nawabs, benign rajas and cruel ones and the British rulers. But Narendra Modi is the first one who truly belongs to the soil of India.

ECONOMICS

Scouting for Jobs

SOME YEARS AGO, the writer introduced a father to the son of an owner-auditor for his daughter. But the father declined because auditing was after all a business and therefore risky. About a year later, the writer received an invitation for the same girl's wedding to a young man who happened to be working for the same auditor. I was later explained that a job was secure while a business had its ups and downs! During the years the writer frequented the districts in Gujarat, he was invariably asked what industry or *udyog* could he help to bring. It was clear that the impression was widespread that the key to fresh employment was setting up industries. The unpopular truth is that a modern manufacturing unit is more an employer of machines and less a giver of jobs to men and women. By allowing for depreciation every year, machinery gets cheaper whereas the employees need to get increments annually. With technology advancing continually, the need for workers per unit of machinery or rather per piece of the product gets less and less. These mindsets, whether with regard to security of a job or the potential of an industry, must be given a go-by.

This is not to say that industry is not necessary for the economy to grow—it is, after all, the foundation of a robust modern economy. But if anyone expects it to provide a great deal of direct employment, he would be disappointed. The indirect jobs in areas like supplies, sales, transport et al would certainly be helpful to the economy and employment. The other threat to jobs is automation that comes with electronics and computerisation. Although not in a big way, yet robots are replacing some workers in factories. Then again, very desirably, more and more women are joining the worker market which makes jobs fewer for men. So much for the second and third or service sectors of the economy.

The government or bureaucratic sector has grown to be very big and is already beginning to reduce or actually shrink. For example, the Posts & Telegraph Department is nothing like the giant it was. And yet, there are millions of young men who may go through life waiting for government jobs. For one, such jobs are traditionally presumed to be secure until the retirement age. For another, private assignments demand qualifications which not every aspirant has. Commerce and industry are yet to be set up in many areas of the country. Then there is the issue of reservations which exclude quite a few sections of the people, be they the Jats, the Patels or the Marathas.

Yet, most politicians again and again promise more and more jobs. Everyone is for economic growth but that does not equal up to the creation of employment as most of the common youth see jobs. What is, therefore, necessary to inculcate is the idea of an economic citizen, a self-engineered way of earning a living—be it as a doctor, lawyer, para-medico, shopkeeper or even a *pheriwala* or a peddler, but not a dependent on anyone for survival. The government's responsibility is to create and sustain the economic environment for the willing self-reliant citizens to have ready opportunity. The government's function is to govern and not provide jobs. The size of the bureaucracy need not exceed the demands of administering the country. The price of a heavy or a top-heavy government would be either high taxes or printing currency leading to inflation. For example, something like 40 per cent of the jobs in France are provided by its government directly or otherwise. How long will the country survive as a prosperous modern state?

A great constraint of the European Union is the Euro which does not allow any of its member countries to devalue its currency. If, therefore, any member cannot keep pace with German economic efficiency, it either has to rationalise or head for impoverishment. The Soviet Union guaranteed full employment and this noble commitment was one of the causes of its eventually going bankrupt in 1992. Moreover, in the course of the twenty-eight years since then, Russia has not developed as an economy. God forbid, if the country had not been gifted with petroleum, what would have happened? A full employment guarantee sterilises the people's aptitude or potential for entrepreneurship. The spirit of economic self-reliance would do the opposite.

To refer back to setting up industries, it should be remembered that this is a globalised world. Almost every manufacturer has to face competition on a potentially global scale. Why not, therefore, also consider promoting institutions that do not have to compete so much, yet at the same time serve the immediate needs of the country? Health and education, apart from employment, are urgent necessities. Hospitals are quite worker-intensive and several thousand of them are needed immediately if the common people's health has to be cared for. The Rs 5 lakh per family insurance scheme inaugurated by the prime minister will also be readily available. PricewaterhouseCoopers in a professional survey has recommended that by year 2034 India would require 36 lakh beds. Today, not even a fraction of these are anywhere in sight. Each hospital would need several hundred non-medical persons and all the hospitals, when ready, should absorb millions indirectly and help to generate many jobs. The medical and para-medical staff would be extra.

If the Right to Education Act 2009 is to be taken seriously, thousands of schools would need to be created. Many of the state schools that exist are more in name and less in function. Some have only a few teachers while in those that have more, the teachers do not attend regularly. The result is that the students that graduate from them are semi-literate. Vocational polytechnics are the demand of the day; not to speak of colleges and universities. Only if these are developed, will the demographic dividend we hear so much about, pay off for the country. And if the institutions were set-up, their capacity to provide employment would be enormous.

Tourism, whether domestic or for pilgrims, is another area of neglect, although it has the potential for enormous, visible employment. The variety of sites to see, monuments to visit and places of worship to pray at in India are numerous. The Himalayas in the north have a potential far greater than Switzerland. The only deficiency is the lack of development and infrastructure. Conquering Mount Everest continues be a craze for climbers; but those who cannot climb can take a jeep to Sandakphu at 12,000 feet and watch the tallest peak as if it was across a very broad avenue. The Kanchenjunga twin peaks are 80 Km as the crow flies from Darjeeling at 6,000 feet. The architectural jewels in Odisha can attract tourists from around the world. The beaches in Puri can potentially match many in the world but where are the facilities to make an American or a European tourist feel comfortable? Keeping aside employment and economics, it is a pity these Indian gems go unvisited, unseen by so many on the globe. South India again is a paradise for tourists and pilgrims but not with the current infrastructure.

Finally, agriculture also offers a great deal of scope provided we teach the farmers not only how to increase productivity but also to upgrade the value of the crops they grow. The late Prime Minister Charan Singh had written in his book *India's Economic Policy,* based on his field experience, how almost infinite is the scope of farming to offer a livelihood to people. Israel has demonstrated how to farm in a desert with the minimum of water. Unilever Ltd, have demonstrated in their large open-air pavilion at Disneyworld near Florida how, for example, 20 brinjals or tomatoes can be grown vertically on four to five square feet of land space. With the many small farms we have, this may be the only way of saving those who are today marginal or even smaller farmers.

Psycho-Economics of Two Cities

SCHOLARS HAVE PROBED not only the psychological influence on economic behaviour but also the psychophysiological effects. There does not appear to have been any attempt to explain why a particular person or the overwhelming majority of his/her community chooses to pursue a particular vocation. The Calcutta of yesteryears offered identical economic opportunities to everyone who came to the three villages of Kalikata, Sutanuti and Gobindapur as they grew over three centuries into a metropolis.

It is incredible how most of the major professions were pursued by specific communities. To start with recent decades, soon after Independence, British owners began disinvesting in their companies, partly due to their apprehensions about Nehruvian socialism and partly due to some violent incidents perpetrated by trade unions in the urban areas. A possible third reason for disinvestment could have been fear of obsolescence of technology after the innovations seen as a result of the world war.

Whatever be the British motives, most of the disinvestments were attractive commercial propositions for Indian buyers. Nearly all of them were bought over by entrepreneurs who had migrated from Rajasthan; there was not a single son of Bengal. The zamindaris had just been abolished and many a wealthy young man should have been on the lookout for an alternative occupation. This was important not only for the young men but also for business and industry in West Bengal. Some local ownership would make the enterprises appear to be 'ours' and not 'yours'. The feeling of 'ours' makes the trade unions view the industry more sympathetically. Why such a cut and dry, black and white picture—only the psychology of economics can explain?

The expert's snap answer may be that the indigenous people of Bengal had not been used to taking business risks. But risks were taken by the people. A father with limited funds often did not hesitate to risk half of it on his son going to England to become a barrister, an FRCS or MRCP or chartered accountant. The boy could come back and his practice might not take off. Is that not risk taking? There had to be some other reason to avoid business, like a landlord considering business an inferior vocation?

An equally interesting phenomenon was that there were reputedly over a hundred thousand people originally from Gujarat residing in Calcutta. Many of them were traders, others were colliery owners and the rest professionals or in private sector jobs. Some traders were wealthy as were many of the colliers. Yet not one of these wealthy entrepreneurs ventured to touch the British bargains. Why? Should not economists explain? Incidentally, members of hardly any other community except the Rajasthanis came forward to take advantage of the opportunity.

Avoidance of business and industry could be attributed to the fertility of the Bengal soil superimposed by the zamindari system which enabled some of the land owners to have leisure. The time and energy this spared helped to facilitate the Renaissance, which in turn could justify the claim 'what Bengal thinks today, India thinks tomorrow'. It should not be overlooked that West Bengal was the leading industrial province on the morrow of Independence. The only snag was that most of the industrialists until then were British. As they began preparing for their departure, the industrial decline started. Unfortunately, the fall was more precipitate than for a state's industrial economy to take a breath and recover. All in all, West Bengal has had to pay a heavy price for many of its people avoiding business and industry.

Trade unions also played their role in bringing down the economy despite being almost invariably honest. Paradoxically, their honesty brought greater problems than they might have otherwise faced. The leaders knew their science, art and craft like the back of their palms. They argued rationally, if not always reasonably. Most of the industrialists could not cope with the unions and unfortunately did not study their side of the art and craft of industrial relations. They did not give the subject the importance it deserved. The result was quite often agitation, strikes, lockouts, unrealistic wages and eventual sickness of many an industrial unit. The biggest of companies seldom had a director who was familiar with industrial relations and left the portfolio to be handled by their labour officers.

Incidentally, human resource experts dealt with executives and not workers. It is for economists to borrow from the discipline of psychology to diagnose the causes of this multi-sided failure at the cost of nearly a hundred million people of the state.

The enigma does not cease at Kolkata. It extends to Mumbai which too is a city founded by the British. King Charles II of England received the group of islands on the Konkan coast as part of a dowry when he married Princess Catherine of Braganza, Portugal, in 1662. The islands grew into a town and then a city called Bombay which, initially, because of being a natural harbour, offered enormous opportunities to whoever wanted to do business and eventually also develop industries. The Parsis came from South Gujarat. The Tatas transferred their ship-building skills and experience to Bombay. They flourished as did the Wadias, the Petits and the Jamsetji Jehangir family in other ventures. Several other Parsis also made themselves into big business houses.

Gujarati banias also followed with their acumen in trading, money lending, broking in commodities etc. rather than manufacture. They made good money, were successful in their respective spheres and gradually became the beams and pillars of Bombay city. The big Parsi business houses were much larger than the bania firms but the latter were more numerous. They followed the Parsis into establishing textile mills as well as other manufacturing. Hoteliering was not a part of their aptitude mainly because of their vegetarian inhibitions. However, they were generous with charities, building hospitals and starting schools and colleges. Then there were the Memons, Khojas and the Bohras who displayed their talent in business. The Muslim contribution to the making of Bollywood was enormous.

Another community which was prominent in the making

of Bombay was the Goan; be it football or hockey, the migrants from Goa were stars. Cricket was not neglected and Anthony de Mello went on to head the Cricket Control Board for years. For long years, the Goans led the catering services of Bombay. Chira Bazar was the mini-Goa of Bombay. But most Mumbaikars naturally belonged to the Marathi-speaking people. The upper classes took to education, both school and college, as well as the government services. As industry and business grew, they also became business executives. The common folk played a sterling role in providing the services as workers, supervisors and officers. All the communities played an active role as creators of what some have called the New York of India.

It is uncanny that each community dominantly played its own different role and seldom competed with another, not to speak of clashing. Why? To an identical opportunity, how is it that each group responded so differently? Something to do with their distinct psyche? Or some other factors? Can the economists please answer? Why have they so long kept silent on the psychology behind different responses to the challenge—whether in Kolkata or in Bombay?

Failure of State Capitalism

IN HIS COLUMN 'Withering Heights', Govind Bhattacharjee (*The Statesman*, 21 January 2019) has highlighted India's most gigantic scam. Privatisation is not its panacea. How many private industrial houses do we have who would be liquid enough to pay and acquire public sector units? And even the liquid ones might not all have the confidence to get involved in units which could be over-staffed. Work culture cultivated in para-governmental organisations would also be difficult to change for many a private management. Whither lies the way out? The writer believes that a beginning would be best made by making all interested Indians aware of why the country embarked on this journey of public undertakings in the first place.

The root reason was twofold. One was the ideological inclination of the then Prime Minister Jawaharlal Nehru whose faith in socialism, whether Soviet or Fabian, made it easy to push state ownership of the means of production. Apart from him and many a leader of the time, the academic environment too was Left leaning. Capitalism was associated with the West as well as imperialism. Many were psychologically anti-West due to the British rule. Marxists, whether Soviet or others, churned out and distributed a great deal of eco-political literature. The capitalist-leaning polities on the contrary took much less interest in propaganda. All in all, in India, it became fashionable to be a socialist. Even top industrialists in Kolkata in their social conversations would not hesitate to say that we all have to be socialist. How else would the better-off people survive in such a poor country?

Such was the growing milieu in which the party in power introduced a socialistic pattern of society at its Avadi session in 1955 as the national policy. There was no significant opposition either by the industrialist classes or chambers of commerce. No political party, except the Bharatiya Jana Sangh (whose present avatar is the Bharatiya Janata Party), had a contrarian view. Jawaharlal Nehru was thus able to unfurl the banner of socialism without any hindrance. From the viewpoint of industrialisation, there were a few resourceful entrepreneurs who in due course did establish large factories but these were for products of their commercial choice. There was hardly anyone with funds, inclination or the know-how to build infrastructural plants, like steel plants. Such contributions had to be made by the public sector funded entirely by the government.

At this point in time, awareness of one particular aspect could have saved the country and its economy, that is that investment and management are two different ball games. In

India to this day, this big difference is not recognised. Almost every entrepreneur believes that his offspring, preferably son, is best suited to succeed him. In most cases, he genuinely does not see the difference. His idea of professional management is to employ managers and give them powers but which are subject to the authority of the family member, who is the chairman-cum-managing director. It is true that over the last two decades there is realisation that non-investment management skills are necessary. But this awareness is still limited in the private sector and even less in the government, where possibly every officer might presume that he is as suitable a manager as he is a bureaucrat.

An officer knows his rules and meticulously follows the procedures; he has no yardstick of performance and can afford not to think about it. His preoccupation would be with how many steps in the ladder of promotion he has climbed and in how many years of service. There are no doubt exceptions, but those are by chance and not by choice of career or training. On the other hand, the average ministry would have no hesitation in placing an IAS officer as chief executive if one was needed, as well as one was willing. It does not matter if procedure overbears profit so long as the rules are obeyed meticulously.

If this could be the flaw at the level of management, lack of accountability is likely to have been the bane at the top. Ministers are liable to change and the secretaries are prone to transfer or eventually retire. In the ultimate analysis, there is no constant factor to ask for answers; unlike the nag of dividend or the return on investment (ROI) beyond the dividend. So long as the auditor passes the annual accounts, he is happy. His is not to question the ROI but only to clarify that the procedure has been adhered to. For him, profit or loss is a matter for the management to worry about. And a Public Sector Undertaking (PSU) has no ultimate, permanent management whose shoe pinches, if not bites, in the event of a loss.

What is the way out of this paradox of the need for results and the paucity of many giant and liquid entrepreneurs? The answer should lie in the president of India not owning the PSUs except financial institutions like the Life Insurance (Corporation), General Insurance Corporation (GIC) or public sector banks. Ideally, however, even these should be inter-held amongst themselves rather than by the president of India. Let the government appropriately fund these institutions, and even more of them if required. Let them be among the shareholders along with the public. And why not foreigners as well as Indians? Let today's PSUs be converted into such corporate entities with professional managers appointed by their shareholders. And leave it to each shareholder being responsible for checking how his corporation has done every three months or so. Let the stock exchanges reflect the performance. The prevailing price of the share would be an important measure of how things are ticking in each PSU, whether central or state patronised.

If the government chooses to give a subsidy or offer a concession for a public cause, so be it. But that must be granted as a sum of money from the state or central budget as the case may be, so that PSUs do not run either as zamindaris or as orphans ending up "as everybody's business is no one's concern".

An example of governmental majority investment and yet the company being run as a commercial venture by professional managers was Larsen & Toubro, until say, three odd decades ago. For years, the public institution held some 54 per cent of the shares but otherwise ran like a normally successful company with hardly any wide awareness of who exactly owned it.

There is no doubt that the country still needs substantial industrialisation, especially of an infrastructural nature. The Ministry of Industries can invite Indian managers of proven record or even successful industrial houses, as well as foreign and multinational corporations of renown, to propose industrial as well as infrastructural schemes. Individual managers, if acceptable, would be asked to invest or find investment of up to 5 per cent, whereas corporations should be expected to find up to 26 per cent investment. Thereafter, if any more investment is required, the institutions should be approached by the promoters.

This would be one way of achieving rapid development without the need of the traditional public sector. With schemes suggested by professional managers of corporations, whether Indian or foreign, and approved in principle by the financial institutions, there should be a safe enough check on the merit of the proposal. The Indian public also joining in to invest would be further reasoning.

Coming to the state PSUs first of all—local governments should be persuaded not to involve corporate or commercial enterprises in welfare or charitable activities. State governments, too, should be discouraged from investing directly in their PSUs. They could develop their own financial institutions, as well as be free to approach central institutions, including public sector banks. Meanwhile, all sick units should be sold and if not saleable, should be closed.

We more or less began this article with an exhortation that investment and management are different ball games. It should be made clear more emphatically that business and politics or ministries must remain separate. They should restrain themselves from interfering with each other. The total losses made by public sector units, state as well as central, as listed by Mr Bhattacharjee, would total up to enormous figures. Add the cost of carrying these losses, and that would be another colossal sum. If only most of these monies had been deployed more constructively, imagine how much more progress the Indian economy would have made?

Gandhi and A System that Worked

THE MORE ONE writes about Gandhi, the more remains to be told. For example, little has been said about his genius for marketing. Without it, possibly, he might not have been able to spread his message of non-violence. We must remember that in his days the media of communication were limited. The most relevant of his legacies is his genius for creating a system for national awareness for freedom.

The finest example of a system that has worked in our country is that of Gandhi. His struggle for India's freedom was an integral package which mobilised the masses, harnessed their political energies and, at the same time, promoted their socio-economic welfare. His discovering among the masses the desire for freedom and establishing his credentials as a super leader were the first links in his system. It is unlikely that so many across the country would have cared to listen to him had he not attained the stature of a mahatma. In our society, a speaker is more important than his speech; a leader matters more than his leadership. Gandhi, with all his wisdom but without his mahatmahood might have been a voice in the wilderness.

To be a mahatma a message was not enough. The message had to be communicated across the subcontinent, to its many towns and villages. There were few highways in those days and most villages were difficult to access. Illiteracy was high and not many read newspapers, most of which were British owned. Languages were many. Even when the radio came in 1927, it belonged to the rulers. And yet, Gandhi cut across all these barriers with the help of the *charkha* and *khadi*. Apart from helping the landless in the villages to earn more, the spinning wheel explained to all Indians what the struggle for freedom was all about. This instrument of communication was more eloquent than any words could have been.

Gandhi was able to achieve mass involvement by espousing the cause of the Dalits. By demonstrating his care for the most downtrodden of society, he was able to convince everyone that his struggle was for the betterment of all Indians. This was yet another link in Gandhi's package. Having inspired the Indian masses, having communicated with and involved them in the freedom struggle, the problem would be to give them the weapons to fight with. Guns were no answer. For one, the British had many more of them. For another, violence would have confined the struggle to some young revolutionaries to the exclusion of common people, old and young, men and women. The fight could not then have been a mass struggle. Gandhi found the answer in non-violent non-cooperation. He invented "*satyagraha*" (insistence upon truth and holding onto it) as a weapon any Indian could wield.

Thus mahatmahood, the charkha and khadi, the cause of the Dalits and satyagraha were all essential links in an integral system. A full package of strategies and weapons that inspired and involved so many Indians together in achieving a national goal. And all this without disrupting general life or unduly hurting any section of its people. If anything, the spinning wheel and the war on Dalits helped to improve the lot of the poorest Indians.

True, Gandhi's was primarily a political mission for a subjugated people. Today's challenge is mainly a socio-economic one. The package, therefore, has to be different. But there is a great deal we could borrow from this unwritten book of Gandhi's genius for a system.

Without this aptitude for marketing, Gandhi might not have attracted virtual worship from so many people. Having said that, effectively he was more packaging and publicity, less a product. Gandhi's first adventure in Indian policy was joining the Khilafat movement. Since he was the only Hindu volunteer of repute, he was made president. Incidentally, Mohammad Ali Jinnah stayed away from the movement. The movement not only failed but the failure came as a big blow to the Muslims in India who reacted by starting a series of riots against Hindus. The first massacre took place in Malabar, then in Kohat of Baluchistan followed by the Sindh riots. Gandhi's advice to the Hindus was that they should stay on and prove their courage by getting killed. Dr BR Ambedkar has written that India witnessed a communal civil war for twenty years between 1920 and 1940.

In 1921, Gandhi launched the Non-Cooperation Movement. It was meant to be strictly non-violent but unfortunately at Chauri Chaura in UP, a group of disgruntled people set fire to the police station and killed all the policemen inside. The incident upset Gandhi so much that he called off the movement. This was the second feather of failure in Gandhi's cap after Khilafat. The third one came when his Civil Disobedience Movement was launched on the arrival of Sir John Simon and his Commission in 1930. What Gandhi did not approve was the absence of Indians on the Commission. But the disobedience did not go far and a cordial Gandhi-Irwin (Viceroy) Pact was signed before long.

Gandhi alone represented the Congress at the Second Round Table Conference in 1931, in London, called by British Prime Minister Ramsay MacDonald. Gandhi claimed that Indians were one except for the British rule. He took a week to prove this unity. He held meetings with the Indian leaders who were attending the Conference. Nothing emerged and Gandhi had to openly admit his failure. When World War II began, the British took it that the whole empire was behind them. The Congress objected, and as a mark of protest, all its ministries in the provinces resigned. The Muslim League got an opportunity in whichever legislative assembly it was present in some strength. In August 1942, the Quit India Movement followed, which resulted in all significant Congressmen being arrested. That lay further space open for the Muslim League which took great strides in preparation for Partition. Searching for Gandhi's political success was like looking for a needle in a haystack. Yet his popularity remained wide and stable.

The widespread impression in India was that Gandhi had won us our freedom. He certainly had brought about awareness among the people that freedom was very important. But in the end, it was Netaji Subhas whose exploits convinced the British rulers that the time had come for them to leave. It was Netaji who had attracted some 50,000 soldiers of the British Indian army taken prisoner by the Japanese in Malaya (now Malaysia) and Singapore who had defected and joined Bose's Indian National army (INA). The rulers in London had noted that if soldiers who had sworn loyalty to the Crown could break their vow, who else could be relied upon to continue to loyally serve the empire? Its administration depended on lakhs of Indian staff and officers.

Inspired by the example of INA, the naval sailors mutinied on the streets of Bombay and Karachi during February 1946. This was the last blow to the Crown which made it decide to quit India. Netaji's contribution was decisive but it was downplayed by the Congress government that followed. Subhas Bose was left to be forgotten. On the other hand, as VP Menon, Advisor to Viceroy Mountbatten said, 'Gandhi lived for Muslims and eventually died for Muslims'.

On the Night Staff

NOTWITHSTANDING THE ECONOMIC progress India has made since 1991, the majority of our people are still poor. As a country, we have more people and fewer assets; which means India should make the fullest use of its assets. But we do not. The organised sector of those employed works, on an average, some 56 per cent of its potential working days. The off-days begin with Saturdays/Sundays, festivals/national holidays plus privilege, casual and medical leave. On an average, a working day equals say eight hours and the remaining sixteen hours are spent in other activities including sleep and rest. Be that as it may, but it must be remembered that every holiday may be fun for the employed but a wage denial for the daily wager and the casual worker; more so because there are so many holidays.

In fact, it is cruel for them. For some reason, they have not protested and no one has helped to voice their grievances. On the other hand, millions in India are unemployed or have very little to do which earns an income. In the bargain the society, by giving itself so many holidays, impoverishes its members in large numbers. The intention here is not to whip people into working harder. The plea is that the society as a whole should be enabled to work as hard as possible. For long years, factories have been known to work on a twenty-four hours basis, admittedly split into three shifts. Why cannot all or most vocations attempt to work on a similar basis? Wherever practicable, the State should encourage establishments to work round the clock. Perhaps, to begin with working hours should be extended. To make such extended hours possible, the State must ensure zero-exception and law and order. Efficient policing would be only the beginning. Also, there could be a wider range of available jobs, as a lot of job openings are solely intended for workers open to shift work. If one starts taking them into account, the pool of jobs available naturally widens.

Deterrence, or in simple terms fear of the law is very important. In the endeavour to achieve such fear, the judiciary must play an active role. Quick justice is essential. Continual vigilance by police vehicles seen to be patrolling should be effective in arousing confidence among the citizens, women as well as men, willing to go to work even at night. In the east, the *barats* traditionally were confined to very few close male relatives so that the ceremony could be performed behind closed doors. The custom had little to do with religion; in south and western regions, weddings are held during daytime as there is less fear of abduction or attack. If law and order is guaranteed, time of day or night could be chosen as per need or convenience and not out of fear.

Just think of the Scandinavian countries like Norway, the land of the midnight sun. For half the year there is more of light than darkness and the other half more darkness than light. Regardless of the time of year, work and rest go on as usual. We, in India, should also get over the mind-set that day is for work whereas the night is more or less for rest. This essential change would come if work places like offices, shops, law courts, et al are seen working overnight albeit with different sets of working people. Courts should make the beginning because there are lakhs of pending cases at every level, from the Courts of Small Causes to the Supreme Court. Nor is there a dearth of lawyers looking for more work. The objective of this suggestion is that eventually there would be two or three sessions or shifts of work wherever there is scope. The same assets like buildings would be utilised for more hours, there would be employment for more people and, in turn, they would help to expand the economy or GDP.

Coming to the climatic conditions, India is overall a warm country. True, the hills are cooler and colder; so are the plains of north India during the winter. Nevertheless, we look forward to the winter in preference to the other months, whereas the whole of Europe yearns for the spring and summer. In many parts of Europe, often the nights are unbearably cold while on the plains of north India days in the summer can be scorching hot. Every year during the month of May, Churu in Rajasthan touches 50 degrees centigrade. Incidentally, as a generalisation, in India the difference between day and night temperatures averages 10 to 15 degrees centigrade.

With the earth warming, it is not impossible that temperature levels would rise further across the country. If that were to happen, willy-nilly, people in all warm countries would have to look for the night to work and the day to rest. In a number of countries in West Asia like say UAE, at the height of summer, offices and other work places start early, close at 12 noon and reopen at 4 pm. Then they carry on working until 8 pm. The writer recalls a trade union leader in Kolkata years ago saying that in our hot climate few workers can actually work for more than three to four hours a day. This was said in the context of someone mentioning that in Germany during the post-World War II years, people worked in a concentrated manner for twelve hours a day to achieve their economic miracle. When Piyush Goyal was Power Minister in the first Modi government, he had declared that India was power surplus. The obstacle now was the deficiency in the distribution network. Air-conditioning is not only expensive but also generates heat and is, therefore, undesirable in a climate of global warming. In any case, the submission here is of gradually moving towards two or three shifts over twenty-four hours. We need to occupy and employ double to treble the number of people.

Cricket is a useful example of how night can partly or fully replace day. The first step was to attract more spectators. The next was to persuade the stadiums to install proper lighting. The colour of the ball changing from red to white to pink was the least of the problems. Nevertheless, cricket took a long time to convert; the practice of late evening games was prevalent in football for long years. The likely reasoning was that football in England was a winter sport; which meant the 100-minute game had to finish by 4 pm and there were many clubs as well as matches. Cricket, involving much more time, should have caught on to the football idea earlier. The mindset might have been the problem; plus in England, the working class mostly did not patronise the game. Football was their favourite.

Benefits of Emigration

OUR YOUNG MEN and women migrating to other countries should not be looked upon as a brain drain, which has hitherto been the term used to describe the overseas residence of Indians. The term Indian Diaspora is a generic one to describe the people who migrated from territories that are currently within the borders of the Republic of India. It also refers to their descendants.

The diaspora is currently estimated to number over eighteen million, composed of NRIs (Indian citizens not residing in India) and PIOs (Persons of Indian Origin who have acquired the citizenship of some other country). The US is their top destination; in 2017, people of Indian descent made up 1.3 per cent of American population.

The very substantial Indian diaspora has played an

important role in promoting India's interests abroad; they act as its informal ambassadors. This is more so in the fields of culture, education, economic development, health and arts. Indians have emerged as leaders in areas like information technology. Above all, this community can help India by investing in Indian industry and infrastructure to encourage its economic growth.

Many use the term "brain drain" to bemoan the flight of India's talent and calibre to the developed countries of the West. But this fear of a brain drain is misguided. The fact is that a 'brain' sitting in an uncongenial environment can 'drain' away faster than if it goes to a stimulating interference-free environment abroad. It is decades of Nehruvian socialism which has forced the best Indian brains to migrate abroad. The critics seldom appreciate that the emigrants went because of paucity of career scope in India at the time.

It is, therefore, futile to cling to the outdated notion of emigration being a brain drain. On the contrary, the process should be encouraged as one of service to the world. In the past we often approached the International Monetary Fund (IMF) for loans and were grateful for obtaining them. Indian institutions still borrow from the World Bank and the International Finance Corporation, which are subsidiaries. Giving a loan is welcomed but the arrival of immigrants is often seen as infiltration by the host countries. What is required by a modern organised world is a procedure whereby migration is seen as export and import. It should be welcomed by the receiving country and equally by the country whose citizens emigrate; otherwise, unhappiness results.

Such a procedure already exists in a number of, shall we say, importing countries. Canada, for instance, issues a list every year as to the kind of qualified or experienced people the country needs during the following twelve months. The applicants are duly interviewed and those found suitable proceed. One does not hear of hassles thereafter. The immigrants also do not face any problems in Canada. Many others have migrated to Australia, New Zealand and the USA, apart from Canada.

About a decade ago I came across the case of a niece and her family, a total of five. They had obtained resident visas of a country in the Far East. They were good enough for the five to settle in the new country permanently. One afternoon suddenly she phoned me from Mumbai that their passports had got stuck, most probably in Delhi. After a number of inquiries over twelve days, they were found in the embassy visa office of the country from where they were sent to Mumbai post-haste. This was a genuine case of delay but a travel agent later told me that if offered for sale, that set of five passports would attract a price of up to rupees 20 lakhs. That was ten years ago.

Touts hang around the embassies of a number of popular countries, attractive from the viewpoint of migration. Those opportunists who do not have much money but are keen to emigrate, resort to paying the touts to the tune of three or four lakh rupees, which enables their entry into a foreign country sans passports, visas or any documents. This is nothing but the crass equivalent of smuggling. Little wonder they create heartburn between strict immigration departments and the visitors. It is seldom realised that illegal immigration is far more serious than smuggling of goods.

The emigrants, after being well settled in their new country, should gradually turn into informal envoys or ambassadors. If they conduct themselves well in the new country, they would make India be perceived as a cultured country of good people. However, if they misbehave, pick up fights, steal their neighbour's possessions, they would earn a bad name for India, which could be difficult to erase. That is why the home country's foreign affairs department should take care to briefly educate their citizens before issuing passports to them. Similarly, before issuing a visa the embassy of the country to be visited should briefly acquaint the visitor with the essential dos and don'ts of its culture.

The training and education in the local language should be much more thorough for visitors proceeding for a long or permanent residence, than for a casual tourist. From this the point can also be made that population is not uniformly distributed across the different counties of the world. Migration, therefore, is necessary whereby the thickly-populated countries could send some of their citizens to the thinly-populated places like, for example, Scandinavia or Russia. There is a general impression that Europe is thinly-populated whereas Asia is densely-peopled. This may not be so everywhere; yet many an Indian would be ready to migrate there because of its level of prosperity. The key factor should be whether the country targeted has economic potential and whether its population is declining, steady or increasing. Russia should be an attractive proposition except that its culture is unfamiliar to Indians and it is reputed to be extremely cold.

For Muslims, North Africa, stretching from Libya in the east to Morocco in the west may be attractive. Japan's population is declining despite a significant number of its citizens having crossed a hundred years in age. But the country has a strict immigration policy. Australia and New Zealand have a great deal of space although they follow the procedure similar to Canada. The Scandinavian countries are advanced countries but it is a moot point what they must have been like in the pre-electricity decades. Half the year would have been more winter and the other half more summer. That is why Norway is called the land of the midnight sun. With the progress of time and technology, Siberia may offer much greater economic potential.

The Indian diaspora is the most integrative anywhere, and yet does not seek to aggressively or fundamentally alter the host country's culture and way of life. If anything, it only enhances and enriches it. The West fears the growing number of West Asian migrants within its borders. For example, in Switzerland, they demanded special Islamic facilities like eternal graves—each burial to be exclusive on a spot. But Indians are welcome everywhere and are looked upon as role models, especially in the matter of family and cultural values. More significantly, India enjoys a kind of soft power image that even China, despite its long monocultural history, does not have. For example, the Chinese language has not penetrated even a single one of China's neighbours, whereas Sanskrit is venerated universally. So is the case with the Bhagavad Gita, Ramayana, Mahabharata, Yoga, Ayurveda, et al.

Tax Evasion

EMPEROR ASHOKA, WHEN he turned Buddhist, began the practice of spending from the state coffers to promote the new faith. A large number of monasteries were constructed in the public sector. Some of them are still in existence, and are magnificent structures, difficult to forget for those who have visited them even once. The cave monasteries at Karla and Bhaja which can be reached from Lonavala by the Mumbai-Pune highway are truly impressive. The caves at Ellora and Ajanta are masterpieces of sculpture; little wonder that they are world-famous. After decades now, I still occasionally see the Buddha at one of the Ajanta caves, with three faces, in my dreams. One face is smiling; the same head from a different angle is pensive, while the third is palpably immersed in deep thought. Too much praise has been repeatedly lavished to bear repetition here about the frescoes of Ajanta. The money spent on the many caves was debited to the state treasury filled with the help of taxes collected from the citizens of the Mauryan Empire. The taxpayers comprised admiring Buddhists and the Hindus and Jains of Ashoka's domain.

The non-Buddhists resented religion being sponsored at the cost of the state, which in turn had gathered funds from people's hard-earned money. Arguably, one can say that this was the beginning of the phenomenon of tax evasion in India, in a way with silent social approval. With time, evading tax became a practice that solidified into a tradition. The British rulers must have known this and, therefore, did not introduce direct income tax until 1931, only sixteen years short of their final departure from India. After the 1929 Great Crash on the Wall Street and the ensuing world economic slump, there was no choice but to tax those who earned a profit, to contribute to the state treasury. In sharp contrast, merchants minted money during World War II. The scope to raise money elsewhere was exhausted. By 1946, evasion had already reached levels that called for intervention. One afternoon my father came home with two one thousand rupee notes. He had been virtually forced by his colleagues to buy them at Rs 600 each. When he submitted them to his bank the next morning, he was given Rs 1,000 each. That was the result of the demonetization which I saw at the age of nine. We then saw a similar phenomenon when Morarji Desai was prime minister (1977-79). The last demonetization in 2016 was more drastic with the objective of reducing India's black economy, which was widely believed to be some 40 per cent of the total. It has shrunk as a result of the step taken.

From the time of Qutubuddin Aibak in 1206 AD, North

India had to endure foreign rule until 1947, a period of nearly 740 years. Most Indians could not identify with the foreign rulers and felt no obligation to spontaneously pay taxes. During his Non-Cooperation Movement Gandhi exhorted the people not to pay taxes. Where the citizens spontaneously feel that it is their duty to pay—or else how can the country be administered—the situation is different. One has to iterate here that this is not to say that Indians are any less honest than other people around the world. When it comes to dues to be paid in cash, whether in property purchase or any other transaction, one has never heard of the seller being short-changed. It is not often that an individual owing money to another individual backs out. Where many do not show conscience is when the creditor is a corporate body with no human face, especially a government organisation.

The Muslim rulers were focused on *jaziya* but had nothing equivalent of excise duty or income tax. The land revenue was raised through the *subedar* and his local network. The British were aware of the Indian aversion to paying taxes and found their own ways of raising money to run their empire. Excise Duty, Sales Tax and Octroi were their innovations; *zamindars* and *jagirdars* were an indirect approach. They held back direct taxation or income tax until 1931. In contrast, the rulers of independent India, until very recently, lacked understanding. Nehruvian India's obsession with socialism and progressive taxation jacked up the income tax on individuals to over 90 per cent. Tax evasion became an art and a craft as a result, and most sections of the people revelled in them, whether politicians, bureaucrats or segments of business and industry. The virus did not spare even some sectors of education, whether kindergarten, engineering or medicine.

More to the point, hardly anyone was embarrassed to talk of the black economy. In fact, pundits called it the "informal economy" and still do. They even pleaded for taking steps to nurse it through the recession caused by the 2016 demonetization. At a guess, two-thirds of the trading in the country was a part of this informal sector. Way back in 2007 when a slump was predicted for 2008, one such pundit had assured me that nothing much would happen to the Indian economy as long as the informal sector existed. He was proved right; what he did not admit was that the informal sector does not enable the economy to grow. It acts like opium and a lot of the cash gets sucked into non-productive areas; the economy, therefore, does not grow to its potential.

Ideally, every surplus rupee should be invested immediately so that it helps to produce new goods ready for sale. Even better, more money should be either borrowed or even printed by the government (deficit financing) for producing new goods and services. The only precondition is that the new production should be so quick as to be more productive and not be a burden on the economy that causes inflation. The Chinese displayed extraordinary imagination when their government allotted land almost for free, provided loans at one or two per cent interest to acquire the machinery and marked out special industrial zones wherein wages were fixed between the workers and employers. The State thus went a long way to lay out its currency; in return it insisted that (approximately) 75 to 80 per cent of the sale value of exports had to be in hard currency.

Over the years, I have mingled with people of different classes, professions and ideologies. The feedback has been fascinating. Few people realise that the State cannot run unless there is collection of money to pay for its employees—from the president downwards to the humblest peon and *chowkidar*. Then the soldiers, the entire military and all the weaponry have to be paid for. When in Parliament, I witnessed discussions on the Railway budgets, which lasted three to four hours. The most popular aspects were the demand for broad gauge to be introduced in one's constituency, lockable gates at the crossings where there were none and the quality of food served during travel. In a parliamentary session in 1999, the discussion on food lasted for well over two hours. The subject was *halal* and what could be done to help those passengers who did not eat *jhatka* dishes. The arguments went on and on until, about two hours later, it was resolved peaceably that no meat should be served; only vegetarian food be served on the trains for all. The flag of Indian secularism was thus unanimously unfurled. Railway tickets were a purchase like any other and the less one paid, the better it was.

In case of taxes, if one could avoid paying, all the better. The attitude was that when it came to payment of taxes, payment of every rupee was to be avoided if possible. Many a practitioner of the legal profession made a subtle differentiation between tax avoidance and tax evasion. The former was ethical as well as legal. The moral of this entire story is that most Indian people are unaware of the equation between the citizen and the State when it comes to what he/she gets and what he/she should pay and why. The State cannot run without taxes. When Chinese and Pakistani guns boom, what is New Delhi supposed to do? From where are the funds for defending the country to be obtained?

HISTORY

From Nehru to Modi

ON 26 MAY 2014, the Nehruvian era saw• its sunset and yielded the horizon to the sunrise of a Modivian epoch. There were a few socialists left, but the failure of communists to get elected marked the cremation of all shades of socialism. After the break-up of the Soviet Union, the ideology might not have survived. The fact that communists did manage to get elected was a tribute to the strength of the Red party organisations. Secularism was a bogey promoted to prevent a nationalist movement from rising. Uncannily, neither socialism nor secularism was written about in the Preamble of the 1950 Constitution. They were both smuggled into the document during the Emergency in 1975.

Pluralism was another balloon floated to protect family-owned parties against competition that might grow out of the soil of India. India, after Partition, did not need a pluralistic polity. Yes, there was a substantial Islamic presence but it was meant to end with the creation of Pakistan or the New Medina. For the rest, India has a single thread binding its ethos. That is the faith in karma and its fruit or *bhagya*. Aldous Huxley called his book *The Perennial Philosophy* possibly because karma is as scientific as physics. That every action has a reaction equal and opposite, explains why India has not disintegrated, whereas Islam could not hold Pakistan together beyond twenty-four years. There are other religions in India and they have a right to flourish, but a State cannot be structured to suit every minority. The writer has come across many Indian Christians who do not reject the role of karma in life; one reason why they spontaneously mingle with the mainstream politics and never betray symptoms of separatism.

To divert attention and perpetuate dynastic rule, slogans were necessary. Indians cannot digest socialism because it pretends to stand for equality, which militates against liberty which is a corollary of karma. Every individual's actions are different so one cannot put a lid on virtuous karma of anyone. Excellent deeds should yield excellent destiny, which would make equality an illusion. Similarly, the Hindu ethos is replete with so much tolerance that it makes secularism redundant. There is no element of politics in Hindu scriptures and India has accepted almost everyone who has come to settle here. This is a compliment which every Jew the writer has met has paid the Hindu ethos. Hinduism itself is so full of plurality and variety that pluralism is also redundant.

Nehruvianism, according to Jawaharlal himself, could not have been native to the Indian soil. He himself is reported to have proudly stated: "I am a Muslim by culture, an

Englishman by upbringing and a Hindu by accident". The preceding paragraphs have illustrated how alien and contrived Nehruvianism was. This explains two things: one, the slowness of India's development; the situation was rather like making Indians function with their right hand thrust into a left hand glove. Two, inevitably, there was a wide gulf between Nehru's India and the real Bharat; little wonder that Narendra Modi has been looked upon as a parvenu in New Delhi. He, therefore, needed to be elected a second time with an increased majority for India to accept him as its ongoing leader.

If we were to compare India's stature in the world when Dr Manmohan Singh was prime minister to what Narendra Modi was able to achieve in a matter of three to four years, the contrast becomes stark. Modi became Prime Minister in 2014, and the following year was invited to address the British Parliament.

Jawaharlal Nehru was put on an unduly high pedestal, and nearly all the policies he followed were treated as an ideology. The Congress party wanted to play down the 1962 disaster at the hands of the Chinese. Indira Gandhi who succeeded Nehru soon enough, was keen to give her father as much importance as possible. Thereafter, whether democracy, socialism or secularism—each was twisted to suit the prime minister at any given time. Indira Gandhi included an Emergency as a part of democracy. Nationalisation of banks and the coal mines were treated as socialism, although the takeover was an act of state capitalism. Minority appeasement was made into an arm of secularism. These ideological distortions distorted policies, which in turn prevented India from coming into its own and progressing at its potential pace. Even as late as 1978 or 1980, the Chinese and Indian economies were at comparable levels. It must be noted here that China was also held down by ideological compunctions. Mao Zedong was succeeded by Deng Xiao Ping, who was a pragmatist par excellence. He famously said: "It does not matter what the colour of a cat is, so long as it catches mice." Thereafter, his country's economy really took off and rocketed to become the world's second largest economy after the USA.

Meanwhile, India was paying the price of Nehruvianism and continued to pay dearly until the advent of PV Narasimha Rao as Prime Minister in 1991. Supreme power had fallen into his lap like a lottery. Yet, midway through his term, he slowed down on his reforms and virtually halted the country's economic progress. Narendra Modi came to power in 2014 with the good intentions of releasing the country's potential towards progress and prosperity. Little had he realised that most nationalised banks had their coffers empty. They had lent out money recklessly during Dr Manmohan Singh's ten years as prime minister. Most of the money was not intended to be repaid by the unscrupulous borrowers.

A great deal of the Modi government's energy was wasted curing this malaise of non-performing assets, rather than investing in due development. Nevertheless, two historic steps were taken—the first was demonetization, which happened to frighten many an operator of the black economy. No modern economy can function or prosper on parallel sledges, namely black money and white. This was followed by the introduction of the Goods and Services Tax (GST). This tax is now virtually the only indirect tax in India, except for items like liquor and petroleum.

This has converted the entire Indian market into one, unlike the days of State sales tax. It has gone a long way in preventing the generation of black money. These were not popular measures with the beneficiaries of black money and, therefore, required an exceptionally bold and strong leader to enforce them. They will stand the Indian economy in good stead for progress and prosperity indefinitely.

The area in which there is likely to be a sharp contrast between the old and the new ethos is foreign policy. Modivianism is unlikely to be passive, unlike in the past when India was perpetually ready to retreat instead of resisting. The cost of foreign policy is largely the expenditure on defence, which has been a neglected area, especially under Nehru himself until at least 1962. The Dr Manmohan Singh period was equally barren. India's image among the world's leading powers has been a great achievement of the Modi government. The standoff at Doklam was a feather in India's cap, whereas the airstrike on Balakot was a glorious moment in the context of counter-terrorism.

On Gandhi

NO ONE IN HISTORY could attract masses of men, women and children on to the streets as Mohandas Karamchand Gandhi. He did this to make Indians aware of the value and meaning of freedom in the days when the means of communication were scarce. There were few newspapers and most of them were controlled by the British. Moreover, illiteracy was rampant and, therefore, the readership was quite small. There was no radio until 1927 when the British government introduced it with the ownership remaining in its control. There were no aeroplanes to fly leaders in Gandhi's time; he had to cover all of India by train.

His attire without even a shirt, and his bamboo stick longer than himself must have conveyed something to the masses, most likely credibility. The *charkha* and *khadi* most effectively conveyed what political freedom could bring by way of the economic relief, especially to the villages most of which were writhing in poverty. He was no orator and yet he could hold the attention of his vast audiences. Even in 1946 after the Great Calcutta Killings, he had the boldness to hold a mass meeting which was attended by thousands. He said something which the people thought was funny and laughed. Gandhi merely had to say in Hindi that it was no laughing matter (*yeh hasne ki baat nahi hai*) and there was pindrop silence within seconds. This was told to me by a friend of my father's quite soon thereafter.

During his first stay in South Africa and, thereafter, as long as Shrimad Rajchandra lived, he was Gandhi's spiritual guide. Unfortunately, Rajchandra died by the time he was thirty-three. Although by profession he was a diamond merchant, from a tender age he was inspired by Jain philosophy. Gandhi had interacted with him much before he left for Durban. His faith in non-violence was inspired by what he learnt from Shrimad Rajchandra. Once from Durban he wrote to his mentor posing a conflict which assailed him. If one saw a poisonous snake approaching, should one try to kill it and save oneself? This would be an act of violence but did one have a choice, asked young Gandhi. Rajchandra wrote back from Rajkot that for a common person it was permissible to try and destroy the snake. But for persons like them, namely Gandhi and Rajchandra who wanted to achieve greater goals in the time beyond this life, it would be best to ignore the snake. If it bit and killed them, so be it, but non-violence must be adhered to.

How much of the advice assisted Gandhi to imbibe non-violence in his system? In 1924, at Kohat, a town in the North West Frontier Province, Hindus were overwhelmed by the Muslim majority and the brutality was widespread. Gandhi's comment was that ideally Muslims should have protected and helped their Hindu brethren. Failing that, the Hindus should retain symbols of their faith, steel their hearts and allow themselves to be killed. To posterity they would appear to be martyrs and heroes of whom mankind, let alone Hindus, would be proud.

Commenting on the massive atrocities in the Malabar (North Kerala) in 1921, Gandhi's comment was that the Moplahs were abiding by their religion. In *Young India* of 29 September of that year, Gandhi wrote: "We have forgotten about dying for our faiths without retaliation. The Hindus must have the courage and the faith to feel that they can protect their religion in spite of such fanatical eruptions". He warned the government against excessive repression of the Moplahs.

Gandhi was so deeply imbued with non-violence that he called Guru Gobind Singh, Maharaja Ranjit Singh, Chhatrapati Shivaji and Maharana Pratap misguided patriots in the *Young India* of 9 April 1925. If he had an opportunity he would have called George Washington, Garibaldi of Italy or Vladimir Lenin too misguided leaders; they had not hesitated to use violence.

Indeed he was a great communicator. To this day many people in many corners of the world admire Gandhi as the apostle of non-violence and peace. This is despite continual communal riots that took place in his time. Dr BR Ambedkar has written that between 1920 and 1940 there was in fact a civil war raging in India. After 1946 it was worse. Credit must be given to Netaji Subhas Bose and his Indian National Army (INA) which frightened the British. They thought if the same virus of revolt spread to all those Indians, civil as well as military, who served the government, how would Whitehall be able to rule India? The point got driven in on the streets of Bombay and Karachi in February 1946 when units of the Indian navy mutinied. Their officers declared they had been inspired by the INA. Gandhism very effectively conveyed what most Indians wanted but it could not drive the fear of God into the rulers which Netaji did.

If Gandhi had not chosen the path of non-violence, he could not have brought out lakhs of people on the streets. If bullets and bombs fly only a few charged-up young men and women would participate in the freedom agitation. All the elderly and women and children would have been advised to stay indoors. From that point of view, without non-violent non-cooperation and satyagraha, Gandhi could not have succeeded. This strategy did convey a message to the British but could not frighten them. Gandhi never asked the government employees, senior or others to go on strike or resign or not work. The British, therefore, could manage Gandhi in contrast to the message of Netaji's Indian National Army, which the Whitehall thought had set a dangerous example.

There were several mysteries about Gandhi which were difficult to understand. One was why did he favour Jawaharlal Nehru who did not get the support of a single Pradesh Congress Committee out of the sixteen in 1946. Sardar Patel was the choice of fifteen of them, yet Gandhi asked Patel to step aside to give Nehru a chance. This rather arbitrary selection contrasts with his capricious neglect of his own sons especially Harilal who turned Abdullah in protest against his father as he was not sent to school until he was much older. Jawaharlal was his favourite virtual son. Or did he favour him because he was younger whereas Patel was much older? And Nehru was modern and could create a good impression of India in the world outside. Moreover, he was from the Hindi belt, politically the heartland of India.

Here is another famous story of Gandhi. In South Africa, Gandhi, the lawyer, lived in Dunbar. Once he had to visit Pretoria and there was no direct train between the two cities. He bought himself a first-class ticket but at Pietermaritzburg station, a white passenger objected to a non-white being in the compartment. Gandhi refused to move and was eventually thrown out on to the platform. This is a well-known humiliating incident. Even on his home ground he was subjected to a worse disgrace by the British Resident Charles Oliphant who ordered his gatekeeper to physically throw out Gandhi from his office. He had come to request Oliphant to not convict his brother Laxmidas for a crime that the Prince of Rajkot had committed. Everyone around witnessed the incident which must have become the talk of the town. All this was before he left for South Africa.

Gandhi suffered several humiliations in a variety of ways during his stay in South Africa. On the other hand, the Muslims, especially Dada Abdullah, his first employer, were consistently kind to him. Possibly subconsciously, he concluded that the British were prejudiced against coloured people whereas Muslims were good and brotherly. If, therefore, Hindus and Muslims unite, they could push out British rulers from India and free the country.

Indulal Yagnik, the most prominent leader of the Mahagujarat Movement (1958-1960) and a highly-respected figure wrote a book called *Gandhiji*. In it he discusses his 1923 experience in jail with Gandhi. Sighting the moon rise on a Ramzan night excited him even more than the dyed-in-the-wool Muslim leader Maulana Mohammad Ali. He fasted like a believer during the day and ate only at night. Yagnik also stressed Gandhi's exploits with the Khilafat movement which he presided over. MA Jinnah had stayed away from this attempt to save the Ottoman Sultan on his Turkish throne and from being removed as the Caliph who was the head of all Sunni Muslims.

Recurrent Deceptions

THE FATE OF Muslims since 1757 AD has been to be deceived. For the Battle of Plassey, Robert Clive of the East India Company had a troop of only about 3,500 soldiers and sepoys to fight against a horde of one lakh commanded by Nawab Siraj-ud-Daulah. Should there have been a question as to who would win? The Company's agents had, however, in advance, arranged with the Nawab's senior most general Mir Jafar to defect on the temptation of being made the Nawab of Bengal if Siraj-ud-Daulah was killed at Plassey or thereafter. The result was the rout of the Nawab's army; the Nawab was chased, rounded up and killed at Rajmahal.

The Bengal Presidency fell to the Company with Mir Jafar as the titular nawab and Clive as the de facto master. Symbolic of the Muslim fall was that, for the first time, Durga Puja in the autumn of 1757 was publicly celebrated in Kolkata with Robert Clive as the chief guest. Until then, all pujas were held behind closed doors so as not to offend the nawabi sentiments. In short, as a result of the deception at Plassey, the Company had brought down the Muslims from the throne to the floor of eastern India, level with where the Hindus had sat for centuries.

After eastern India, it was the turn of Tipu Sultan's defeat and death at Seringapatam in 1799 at the hands of Lord Richard Wellesley. That signalled the end of Muslim rule in South India. The next Muslim back to be broken was at Awadh when in 1856 Lord Dalhousie took over the domain of Nawab Wajid Ali Shah. This was a big blow in north India, especially UP, which had been the Islamic centre of India. The Sepoy Mutiny of 1857 was essentially a revolt by the dispossessed princes of North India, and the old emperor Bahadur Shah Zafar who got roped in by the mutineers. A substantial number of those punished by being hanged to death at Delhi Gate were Muslim. By 1858, the Muslims of India had been dethroned.

Sir Syed Ahmad Khan was an officer of the Company who stood by the British and emerged as the most influential leader of his community until his death in 1898. He took a contrarian view and asked Muslims to support the British rulers who were *Ahl-e-Kitab* or People of the Book and much better than the Hindu *kafirs*. Contrary to the view of the Islamic clergy, he sponsored the study of English and Western science.

To enable Muslims to study these subjects, he established the Muhammadan Anglo-Oriental College at Aligarh which later bloomed into the well-known Aligarh Muslim University. In 1887, he, for the first time, termed Hindus and Muslims to be separate nations. Whether he was right or wrong, the university grew into, as described by MA Jinnah, "the arsenal of Pakistan".

In 1906, the Muslim League was founded at Dhaka (then Dacca) with the Nawab of the area as the patron. He did not hesitate to accept a loan-cum-bribe of one lakh pounds to patronise the founding. As a corollary, the Bengal Presidency was divided; the event was the partition of Bengal in 1905 into East Bengal and Assam, a Muslim majority province and the rest of Bengal. For Muslims, it was an hour of elation but its effect lasted for only six years. In 1911, King George V came to Delhi and annulled the partition. But in Muslim eyes, the British remained better than Hindus with whom they would not unite for the freedom struggle.

In 1935, Mohammed Ali Jinnah returned from London as life president of the Muslim League. He looked for a new goal and a strategy for the league. Poet Muhammad Iqbal in 1930 had proposed a partition within a loose confederation. A few years later, Choudhry Rahmat Ali, a Cambridge scholar, had coined a name for a Muslim Dar-al-Islam—Pakistan. So when in the 1937 elections, the League did not fare well, Jinnah began thinking of a partition of India. On 23 March 1940 at Lahore, he had the Pakistan Resolution passed by the League. The majority provinces like Bengal, Punjab, Sindh and NWFP showed little interest. They had Muslim premiers and generally dominated their provinces. Where Muslims were in a minority, some of them responded, but why one could not guess. Bihar, UP and the business classes of Bombay showed more enthusiasm because they preferred to compete against the Punjabi peasants rather than the Banias, Parsis and Shettys.

In 1945, the Viceroy called a general election at the end of the year and early 1946. Jinnah took to the campaign road and created a whirlwind. He argued that Hindus and Muslims belonged to entirely different cultures and the former would be in a majority. The Muslims, therefore, needed a separate homeland called Pakistan. The argument caught on like wildfire. No one really questioned how UP and Bihar Muslims would benefit; nor did the other provinces like Gujarat or Orissa (Odisha). Pakistan became the craze. The more meetings Jinnah addressed, the crazier it became. How the two wings of Pakistan 1,600 km apart, comprising Bengal and Punjab, would coexist, no one asked?

On 14 August 1947, the green flag was unfurled by the Qaid-e-Azam and the citizens of Karachi shouted with triumph. They did not realise that before long the Sindhis would became a minority in their own beloved city. Nor did the East Bengalis realise that Urdu would be the national language of their new homeland and their beloved Bengali would become the language of their backyard. Jinnah had indeed sold them a mad dream that ended up dividing the Indian *ummah*. If only the Qaid had let them be, an undivided India would be today 40 per cent Muslim with the prime minister being always a *momin*. Nevertheless, the tragedy of gullibility was not over. Gandhi had four sons of his own but his favourite was Jawaharlal whom he had appointed in a manner that led him to the prime ministership. The Congress party wanted Sardar Patel who was told by the Mahatma to step aside. Nehru was in search of a support base of his own. He befriended the Muslims with charm and flattery. He called himself culturally a Muslim; indeed, his wedding invitation card was printed in Urdu. He and his successors made the Muslims feel that they held the veto on Indian policy. Several of them became presidents and vice-presidents. Dr Manmohan Singh called for fifteen per cent of the country's resources to be allocated to them.

Yet, materially the flattery did not bring any Muslim uplift.

Educationally they remained backward with madarsas teaching them religious subjects, which did not help them to get secular jobs. Hence, they still claim to be poor and backward. Their epic of deception was not yet complete. Maulana Maududi, the founder of Jamaat-e-Islam was against Partition and stayed back in India. But, in a matter of months, he suddenly took off to settle in Pakistan. Janaab Khaliquzzaman of Allahabad decided to stay back and Jinnah had him appointed president of the League. He functioned as such but a few months later suddenly left to go to Pakistan and became the president of the League there. Yet another example of deception was that by Huseyn Shaheed Surhawardy, former premier of undivided Bengal. On 10 September 1947, he wrote at length to Khaliquzzaman detailing a strategy for Muslims in post-partition Hindustan. It read as a very sincere letter, but by January 1948 he also took off for Pakistan.

The Two-Nation Theory

LATELY VEER SAVARKAR has been accused in the media of having introduced the two-nation theory. The first author of the theory was however Sir Syed Ahmad Khan of Aligarh University fame. He first declared his view that Hindus and Muslims were two different nations in December 1887 at a public meeting in Lucknow. He again addressed people on the separate nation subject at Meerut in March 1888. Syed Ameer Ali of Calcutta, the first Indian High Court judge, was the next sponsor of this two-nation theory. Yet another public figure to do so was Poet Allama Iqbal in 1930 at the Allahabad session of the Muslim League. He talked of two Muslim nations within the Indian confederation; one in the north-west and the other in the east. Choudhry Rahmat Ali, a scholar at the University of Cambridge, in 1933 innovated the word Pakistan.

Then followed the redoubtable Muhammad Ali Jinnah who detailed the theory at quite some length while sponsoring the Pakistan Resolution in March 1940 at the Lahore session of the League. Jinnah said: Muslims are not a minority; Muslims are a nation according to any definition and they must have their homeland, their territory and their state. The history of the last 1,200 years has failed to achieve unity, India was always divided into Hindu India and Muslim India. The termination of British regime will be the herald of an entire break-up. If Hindus and Muslims are brought together under a democratic system, it can only mean Hindu Raj.

Dr BR Ambedkar wrote a rejoinder with a volume called *Thoughts on Pakistan*, published in 1941. A quotation would speak volumes for his patriotism and his vision. He began by viewing Partition first from the angle of defence. "The Indian army was predominantly Muslim in its composition", he wrote. "Russia or Afghanistan, the borders of both touch the borders of India. Suppose the Afghans singly march on India, will these gate-keepers (army) stop the invaders or will they open the gates and let them in? This is a question on which every Hindu must feel assured. Attention must be drawn to the stand taken by the Muslim League that the Indian army shall not be used against Muslim powers. This principle was enunciated by the Khilafat Committee long before the League".

Ambedkar also looked at the question of division from the viewpoint of finance. He found that the Hindu majority provinces raised taxes that totalled nearly Rs 52 crores, whereas the Muslim ones earned a little over 7 crores only. "The Hindus have a difficult choice to make: to have a safe army or a safe border. In this difficulty, what is the wisest course for the Hindus to pursue? Is it in their interest to insist that Muslim

India should remain part of India so that they may have a safe border, or is it in their interest to welcome its separation from India so that they may have a safe army"?

In Savarkar's own words, "Several infantile politicians commit the serious mistake of supposing that India is already welded into a harmonious nation, or that it could be welded thus for the mere wish to do so. These, our well-meaning but unthinking friends, take their dreams for realities. It is safer to diagnose and treat deep-seated disease than to ignore it. Let us bravely face unpleasant facts as they are. India cannot be assumed today to be a Unitarian and homogenous nation, but on the contrary, these are two nations in the main, the Hindus and the Muslims in India". He insisted that there were two nations, one Hindu and one Muslim.

Jinnah wanted India to be divided into two, Pakistan and Hindustan; the Muslim nation to occupy Pakistan and the Hindu nation to occupy Hindustan. Savarkar, on the other hand, insisted that although there are two nations in India, it should not be divided into two parts. The two nations should dwell in one country and live under the mantle of one single Constitution. The Constitution could be such that the Hindu nation would be enabled to occupy a predominant position that was due to it and the Muslim nation made to live in the position of subordinate co-operation with the Hindu nation. In the struggle for political power between the two nations, the rule of the game which Savarkar prescribed was to be one man one vote, whether Hindu or Muslim. In his scheme a Muslim was to have no advantage which a Hindu did not have. Minority was to be no justification for privilege and majority was to be no grounds for penalty.

Savarkar further held that the State would guarantee the

Muslims defined measure of political power in the form of Muslim religion and Muslim culture. But the State would not guarantee secured seats in the Legislature or in the administration and, if such guarantee were to be insisted upon by the Muslims, such guaranteed quota was not to exceed their proportion to the general population. Thus, by confiscating its weightages, Savarkar wanted to strip the Muslim nation of all the political privileges it had secured so far. Ambedkar's comment was that this alternative of Savarkar to Pakistan had about it a frankness, boldness and definiteness which distinguished it from the irregularity, vagueness and indefiniteness which characterised the Congress declarations about minority rights. Savarkar's scheme had at least the merit of telling the Muslims, 'thus far and no further'.

Veer Savarkar also felt that the Hindus and Muslims were different people with distinctly separate ethos. Nevertheless, the country did not need to be divided; it could remain one and it should continue to be one, he believed. The rights and privileges, including votes, should be equal. At the same time, the tune of the Indian polity should be called by the Hindus. He had been candid enough to begin his thesis on this subject by declaring that the *punyabhoomi* and *pitribhoomi* of the Christians and Muslims were not in Hindustan, they were overseas. This country, therefore, was Hindu first and everything else later. How exactly did he propose to reconcile the two opposites? On the one hand, Savarkar wanted equal rights for all and, at the same time, Hindus to control the country's destiny. Under no circumstances did he accept the idea of a division of the country.

From the beginning of the twentieth century, Savarkar had seen how defensive the Congress had been and how ineffective the Hindu Mahasabha was in curbing the Muslim aggressiveness, especially after Jinnah had taken complete charge of the League on his return from England in 1935. Possibly, Savarkar's love for the country blinded him to the reality that separate nations had to live separately. True, until 1941 or even until 1946, no one had witnessed the rioting and the violence the League unleashed. *Satyagraha* was no match for Jinnah's Direct Action. As the years have unfolded after Independence, sparks of separation have not disappeared. Even the holy land that was Pakistan split into two within twenty-four years of its birth. Neither Jinnah nor Savarkar realised that Islam has never believed in a nation and cannot hold it together. It is eminently a binder of the entire *ummah*. Lately, in even that function it is shaky. First the Ahmadiyyas were expelled and now the Shias are becoming persona non grata.

Philosophy of Religion

THE DISTINGUISHED IDEOLOGUE Karl Marx wrote that communism was from each according to his ability, to each according to his need. Human needs are about equal, he presumed. Evidently, he focused on physical needs. But what about intellectual, emotional, and above all, motivational needs? Surely, human beings differ so much from one another. The Marxian fixation was so much on the material that he overlooked most other facets of life. After all, he became famous for his thesis on the materialistic interpretation of history, which along with his masterly critique on capitalism, forms the substance of his magnum opus *Das Kapital* (The Capital). The ideology and practice of communism had a short life, less than a century, largely because of Marx's inadequate understanding of human nature; he forgot the old adage that man does not live by bread alone. In sharp contrast, Prophet Muhammad was a genius when it came to psychology. In a man's world, he gave him all the basics he could have wanted—as many women as he wanted, as many slaves as he could capture and maintain, as much land as he could conquer and keep as *wakf* forever and study as much as he liked or as little as he cared for. As a result, Islam was expanding in numbers even fourteen centuries after its birth. Now that the man's world is ending and women are rising, Islamic bigwigs would have to discover new responses to the challenges of modernity.

To Karl Marx, capitalism would have been, "from each according to his ability to each according to his wealth". The Bible had clarified by stating "give unto God what is His and unto Caesar what is his". It logically followed that the leaders of Christianity meant to let the trader pursue his vocation as he wished. This original distribution of functions gave the religion of Jesus Christ the versatility civilization requires to keep growing and flourishing. Unlike Islam, which retained a stranglehold on its followers (for example, apostasy is punishable by death), Christianity gave freedom to its believers and, therefore, could scatter into many denominations. Nevertheless, Christians have respected their faith—that God made Man equal but the vagaries of society makes him unequal. To make up, Christians promote more charities, hospitals, schools, universities et al than any other community.

Socialism, a favourite ideology of many a political party, was defined by Marx as, "from each according to his ability to each according to his opportunity". There is justice personified in this ideology. Ability is god-given but the society must give every member an equal chance to flower and blossom; not keep anyone down or at a disadvantage. The question is how consistently has socialism been practised in many places?

Any ideology that emanates from Hinduism must have at its core the actions and their reactions of every *jeevatma* or soul whether in the current *janma* or life or an earlier one. Karl Marx could have defined it as, "from each according to his karma to each according to his *bhagya*". The destiny of each soul would be determined by the deeds of that soul, whether in this life or a previous one. Conceptually, it is similar to a foundational principle of physics that for every action, there is an equal and opposite reaction. It embodies unquestionable justice as well as science at its precise best. Perhaps, the only imponderable is the Hindu theory of *sanskara* or the transmigration of souls from one birth to another. It is ultimately a challenge of faith. The writer's own experience has been that approximately three-quarters of his life has been an equation of karma and *bhagya*. The remaining quarter is a matter of faith in the karmas of his previous lives or births. He hopes that if three-fourths is true, why not the remaining quarter? Even the most dedicated scientist lives on some faith at least.

The question of faith leads us to the fact that Abrahamic religions are far more demanding than Hinduism. The latter relies on karma or one's own deeds and the resulting reward or punishment, whereas the former insists on the follower accepting Jehovah, Jesus or Allah as the only god of that religion. The slight difference is that Jesus Christ is looked upon as the son of God rather than God himself. There is no variation permissible in adherence to these godheads. The theology of Judaism is not known to have varied since its beginning. Islam disapproves of variations; *ijtehad* or reinterpretation was prohibited about a thousand years ago, after which *taqlid* or orthodoxy has been the way of Islam. Christianity has permitted differences from as early as the fourth century AD, when the Orthodox Church was founded in Constantinople, as distinct from the Vatican. The Reformation began in the sixteenth century, since when the Church split into dozens of denominations.

Essentially, these three Abrahamic religions would be categorised by the discipline of logic as deductive. The basic premise is enunciated in the *Torah*, the *Bible* and the *Quran*. The rest of what is right or wrong flows from the premise like the corollaries of deductive logic. They are consistent and make life easy to lead for the follower, if he is faithful. The discipline is like "Yours is to do or die but not to question why". The premise is given, the corollaries are logical and an undue violation would be treated as apostasy.

The Abrahamic religions, we have seen, are deductive in their logic. They begin with a premise and work downwards. On the other hand, the Hindu view is inductive in its logic, which moves from facts on the ground upwards till it reaches a conclusion. To illustrate this difference, let us suppose that four Hindus happen to meet and each one of them is from a different corner of the country. The person from the Punjab happens to declare roses to be red; the man from Tamil Nadu says he has seen only white roses while the one from Bengal disagrees, for he has seen only yellow roses while the Maharashtrian knows of only pink roses. They might argue for a while and unable to agree unanimously, they would agree to disagree saying, "maybe roses are so in your part of the country". They do not fight or quarrel. On the other hand, an Abrahamic may declare the rose alien to him as a weed or perhaps a flower other than a rose. That is a deductive attitude based on the premise that the colour of a rose is only red. The inductive approach of the Hindu would accept that the ground reality elsewhere could be different and hence, agree to disagree. One of the four could say that he has seen only yellow roses, but maybe in the other areas of the country there are other colours.

On the other hand, Hinduism does not have a book as its fountain of belief; there is no premise, therefore, no corollaries which a follower can refer to, or a commandment or guidance. Nor do Hindus have an ecclesiology or a network of clergy or bureaucracy, either for worship or for administration. There are a few groups of temples, but mostly each one is an independent entity with its own priests connected with no other. As is well known, there are numerous deities and avatars which Hindus worship. In other words, other than karma, Hinduism has no uniformity or a unity of worship. In fact, Hinduism is a paradise of diversity. That is why it is not a religion but a way of life merely anchored on karma and, of course, a few broad groups like the Shaivites, Vaishnavas, Shaktas et al. Half the time, the worshippers are not even aware which group they belong to. One outstanding feature of the faith is its reverence for female deities, whether Durga, Kali, Lakshmi or Saraswati and many others.

Identity and Nationalism

TO THE WRITER, the nation has always seemed a mega version of his home and his family. For a Hindu, his caste has, over the centuries, been the next horizon. In this context, he has considered his faith as personal and by no means anything like a fence or a dividing line between him and the universe. For example, in Gujarat, a Vaishnav marrying a Jain is not unusual. The staunchest Sikh would not bat an eyelid before proposing to a Hindu girl, if all else were equal.

The Abrahamic religions with their origin in West Asia are kept at a distance. For the rest, faith was personal whereas other horizons were socio-political. The subcontinent is still referred to as the country. On the other hand, Pakistan, the New Medina, was allowed to separate without any effort at persuasion. The reported brutality inflicted by General Tikka

Khan on his own brother citizens was unprecedented. Yet, when for the first time, Pakistan lost to Bangladesh in cricket, their then captain Wasim Akram was casual enough to say, "After all, we have lost only to our Muslim brothers".

On the other hand, the pain in Hindu hearts is reflected in the Rashtriya Swayamsevak Sangh remembering every August 14 with grief, as Akhand Bharat Diwas or Undivided India Day. If this is the value that Pakistan attaches to its holy land, let me ask them why they don't suffer a single whisper of sorrow for leaving behind a large number of Muslims in an "unholy" land, which for them is India? In Arabic, India would be called Dar-al-Harb by the Muslims, or the land of conflict. This is happening to the Pakistanis because they have not thought through their conception of nationalism. This confusion is illustrated by the way Pakistan has twisted and turned the facts of its own history.

Otto von Bismarck, Chancellor of Germany during the latter half of the nineteenth century, with valour and imagination had unified Germany by 1871. Some twenty principalities were brought together into one country. Most Germans were proud of this achievement. Yet, they reconciled themselves to their bifurcation after World War II. However, none of the seven West Germans this writer met over the years expressed any enthusiasm for reunification. Publicly, no move, demand or agitation for a coming together has been on record. Three of the seven German gentlemen I met were frank enough in admitting that they hated communists more than they loved their Prussian brethren. This meant that the fear of ideology superseded the pull of nationhood.

Is nationalism a person's search for a larger identity? It is easy and comfortable to be small or moderate. But a larger identity is likely to be more satisfying, whether for the human pride, political influence or economic benefit et al. If the family remains one and motivated, there are greater chances of its becoming successful. However, unity is not always easy to sustain. All the factors and forces that work against it can be suspected of anti-nationalism.

The first such force was Judaism. The Jews love their religion; it is one faith which in early times had an outstanding prophet called Moses. The scriptures that happened to be written by this great man are the holy scriptures for the Jews. Collectively, these scriptures are called the *Torah*. Early Judaism did face enemies, namely from Mesopotamia and others, but a comprehensive threat to it emerged gradually as Christianity grew century by century to dominate Europe. As it happened, this religion of Jesus contributed to the flowering of nationalism. The ruling elite of the nationalist states were often adversarial to Judaism as potentially anti-Christianity. The result was that in order to remain united, Judaism turned supranational. Chaim Weizmann, a prominent Jewish leader, has defined supranationalism as: "There are no American Jews, no Russian Jews, no British Jews, no French Jews, and no German Jews; there are Jews in America, Jews in Britain, Jews in France, Jews in Germany, Jews in Russia..." Weizmann persuaded the British government through its foreign secretary Lord Arthur Balfour in 1917 to announce that the Jews would be allotted a homeland in Palestine before long.

The second great supranational factor is Islam and the Sunnis, who put their faith in what they call the *ummah* (world community of Muslims). The Sunnis comprise approximately 90 per cent of all Muslims. Sir Syed Ahmad Khan, the first post-Sepoy Mutiny Muslim leader, was clear that Muslims were separate from the Hindus and he was anxious to keep his community away from any nationalistic tendency or sentiment. He also exhorted his followers to stay away from the Congress, which had begun promoting Indian nationhood.

The poet Allama Iqbal was more emphatic on the subject of nationalism. After his stay in Europe, he apprehended that due to the collapse of four empires at the end of World War I, many new nation-countries had blossomed. They might well pose a threat to Islam in general, especially in India, with Britain being the connection. He critiqued the idea of nationalism questioning its sanctity, and started moving towards the transnational Muslim community. Iqbal expressed his staunch opposition to the idea of nationalism in the following couplet: "Country is the biggest among the new gods! What is its shirt is the shroud of religion".

The next supranational movement was Marxism. In fact, Karl Marx was clear that the nation-state is an instrument in the hands of the bourgeoisie, the industry-owning and land-owning rich. They were looked upon as the exploiters of the working class and therefore had to be liquidated. Communism thus pitted the classes against the masses, bringing about effectively a civil war, which is suicidal, unless brought to an end quickly.

The Soviet Union, the erstwhile Czarist Empire thus ensured its own break-up in a matter of decades. Of the other two supranational forces, Judaism has lasted long, although at a shrinking pace. Islam, on the other hand, has shown all signs of vigour, although along the way it has aroused a great deal of resentment. By now, it has clashed with non-Muslims from all the continents of the globe except South America. Muslims have made Europe almost an embattled continent.

This is not to say that supranationalism is the only adversary of a well-knit, united nation. Pakistan broke up in 1971 because the Bengali-speaking East Pakistanis could not co-exist with the Western wing indefinitely. One could call this antithetical to national identity. Neither Islam nor Urdu nor the Muslim League could keep the Pakistanis together as one nation, as virtually all separatist leaders from Sir Syed Ahmad Khan downwards had taken for granted. Even the presence of 30 per cent Hindus (in 1947) did not help East Bengal from remaining united with Pakistan. Another example would be that of Slovakia separating from (the former) Czechoslovakia. A few years earlier Yugoslavia broke into several pieces, contemporaneous with the Soviet Union. The saga of the USSR splitting into sixteen republics in 1991 is well known.

Christianity bypassed supranationalism because it allowed itself to follow slightly differing theologies. The sixteenth century Reformation gave Protestant churches a free play. In a number of cases, the monarch led the free play. For example, Henry VIII led England into the Anglican Church and broke away from the Vatican. In the German principalities, the monarchs chose the denomination preferred by their people. The earliest example was that of the fourth century transfer of the Roman capital from Rome to Constantinople (now Istanbul). The emperor and his family were instrumental in setting up what is now called the Eastern Orthodox Church.

One Script (Not One Language)

INDIA HAS CHASED the shadow of a national language long enough. It is time we thought of an alternative which is more effective and easier for all to accept. We could have a common script instead of one of our languages getting more importance, as Hindi has been. More than that, upstaging Hindi means putting the non-Hindi people at a clear disadvantage. If I were a Gujarati, I would have to learn three languages while the Bihari need not go beyond knowing his own mother tongue plus English. Recommending that everyone should learn three languages, like the Bihari to know Tamil too, does not go far. If this is a serious wish, it is a pipe dream.

A pragmatic approach would be to begin by travelling on highways. A Hindi-speaker crossing from Bihar to West Bengal would cease deciphering the road names that are painted in

Bengali. A Tamilian when he crosses into Kerala would face the same problem. A common script should overcome this difficulty. Thus far, the English or Roman alphabet has filled this role of a script. For some mysterious reason, all drivers seem to be able to read signboards and vehicle number plates that are painted in English. That is why the Centre had asked the states to paint number plates of motor vehicles in English letters. To make sure that this instruction was followed, all private car number plates were required to be in English letters painted in black on white, while commercial vehicles were to have the numbers in yellow on black. Regional letters were disallowed for vehicles.

Kakasaheb Kalelkar, the scholarly freedom fighter, had studied this problem in-depth and concluded that after Independence we should begin with a common script and not a common language. After offering his reasons, he had concluded that the Gujarati letters were the clearest and also did not belong to a majority of people. That would avoid any resentment against a majority. However, that was over seven decades ago. We could take a fresh view now. And might we zero in on the Roman alphabet? Such an experiment was tried in the army when Hindustani was written/printed in this alphabet for British soldiers to learn the language. The same way, British youngsters who came to serve in the government or in commerce were taught elementary Hindustani. Incidentally, Gandhi favoured this idea; some alleged that it was because the Muslims approved of it. But this allegation need not be taken seriously.

What should be stated is that Urdu has many letters to pronounce. It has four Zs whereas the other Indian languages have none. Urdu also has two Ks, two KHs, two Gs and so on. The reason is that the language has taken all its verbs from *khadi boli* or Hindi, while its nouns and adjectives are from Arabic, Persian and a few also from Turkish. The word Urdu itself means army in Turkish. On the other hand, the English alphabet has at least two sizes for every letter, capital and the lower case. That would enable the user to accommodate many more sounds. Moreover, Gujarati and Marathi have two Ls while many of the other languages have two Ns; N and n, for example, would solve the problem.

Another advantage of the English script would be that the children would simultaneously be ready to learn, type and write the English language. It has by now ascended to the position of a universal tongue including the lingua franca of the Internet. Moreover, the alphabet is not merely English but also includes all the West European languages, be it Spanish, French, German, Italian, Polish et al. It is only when we reach the Slavic or East European area that the Cyrillic script takes over. Looking ahead in time, there is a possibility that the Chinese and Japanese tongues may one day shift to the Roman alphabet. These Oriental languages do not have a script but only pictographs. Each thought, idea or item is represented by a picture.

A Japanese scholar told me that one could make do with knowing five thousand pictographs but a scholar knows up to 50,000. The Chinese alphabet system is said to contain 100,000 pictographs or symbols, though one could get by with knowing 3,000 to 5,000 of them. One can imagine how easy or difficult this proposition is. And would not thinking be more difficult with pictographs than with an alphabet? So much of the mind would have to divert its attention to remembering the pictographs before thinking can begin. I do feel that maybe one day such languages could shift to the alphabet.

In India, we must remember that a voluntary beginning with a single script should evoke no resistance. At most, incentives could be offered. If in a school there are five divisions, one of them could teach in the single script and its pupils be charged a distinctly lower fee. No force or compulsion need be brought into play. A great benefit of this experiment of a common alphabet would be that when accepted, a major barrier between Indian languages would be demolished. When so many of our tongues get ready to mix, what an enormously rich Indian tongue would emerge! It would indeed be a Great Indian Language. The rest of the world would also find it easier to learn it because of its script. It would no longer be a barrier to cross. The learner would plunge straightaway into the language itself. In other words, Indians would not only come spontaneously closer to one another but also move closer to the rest of the world without even trying!

In all likelihood, this proposition is likely to run into opposition. My Urdu teacher reacted by stressing that *rooh* or soul of the language would perish. My response to him was that the Urdu script was almost the same as Persian, whereas more Urdu speakers in India were closer to the Arabic world. Yet they have not raised any objection.

Many a Bengali or Tamilian and several other linguists would protest against this dilution of their respective scripts. They would feel justified in doing so. However, the question is the richer a language like Bengali or Tamil, the greater is likely to be its contribution to the growth of the greater Indian language.

Pakistan

AS SWAPAN DASGUPTA in his column 'Usual Suspects' in the *Pioneer,* Sunday, 16 August, rightly concluded, the fact of India's partition in 1947 cannot be put back. I would add that the population being one-fourth Muslim (of the then undivided subcontinent) the division was inevitable, even if all the Hindu leaders of early 20th century had been studded with wisdom. The State and politics are an integral part of Islam, unlike other religions. The Constitution of Pakistan, beginning with the first written in 1956, followed by the ones of 1962, 1963 and 1981, all begin with the words "Whereas sovereignty over the entire Universe belongs to Almighty Allah alone, and the authority to be exercised by the people of Pakistan within the limits prescribed by Him is a sacred trust".

From the days of Sir Syed Ahmad Khan, the founder

of the Aligarh Muslim University (AMU), there was talk of Hindus and Muslims as two separate *qaums* or nations. Sir Syed in his speeches at Lucknow in 1887 and Meerut in 1888 unequivocally spoke of Hindus and Muslims as distinct nations. Syed Ameer Ali, a judge of the Calcutta High Court, too, had written on Muslims' separateness. Poet Allama Iqbal of the Muslim League at its 1930 Allahabad session proposed separate political entities. And in 1934, Choudhry Rahmat Ali, a Cambridge scholar and Pakistani nationalist coined the word 'Pakistan'.

It was the Muslims of Uttar Pradesh who were most enamoured of a separate state. However, the only segment that had thought through the idea of separation and its consequences were Bombay's Muslim businessmen.

Jinnah even convinced the Muslims of the minority provinces, specially UP, Bihar and even the composite Bombay, areas which could not have been parts of Pakistan. Muslim-majority provinces of Punjab, NWFP, Sind and Bengal fell in line later, less than two years before Partition. Many students of the Aligarh University went to Punjab to canvas for the League in the 1945-46 elections. They were asked by the potential voters what was there in Partition for them. Their answer was: "To create a new Medina".

Muslims in the subcontinent were approximately 25 per cent of the total population, and distinctly less educated than Hindus, Christians and Parsis. They did not own many industries, nor did they control business to any significant extent, except in Bombay. Whatever there was of Muslim wealth was in land, which the Congress party and its socialists were threatening to take over for the tillers of the soil. Thus, the community, in the foreseeable future, was disadvantaged compared to others.

It was easy to convince the gullible that for the Muslims the choice was "separate or perish". The clarion call "Islam is in danger" was convincing and indeed resonated with them throughout India. Without being able to address crowds in Urdu, Punjabi, or Bengali, languages most Muslims understood, Jinnah could sell this dream. A report by a young Pran Chopra, who later became editor of *The Statesman*, is telling. At Jalandhar, Chopra was present at an election rally in which Jinnah, who was campaigning for the 1945-46 elections, spoke in English. When the *muezzin* called for prayers, Jinnah stopped and sat down on a chair while the crowd dispersed for *namaz*. He lit a cigar and relaxed until the crowd returned, and then resumed his address. Jinnah had no inhibitions about smoking in presence of a gathering of the *ummah*, who did not mind in the least. They saw in him the leader who could rally the *qaum* and lead it to its cherished goal of carving out a new Medina thereby escaping the clutches of what they feared would be Hindu rule. His smoking, pork-eating and wearing Western suits did not matter to them.

The argument merits scrutiny, no doubt. We in India celebrate anniversary after anniversary of India's independence every 15 August. A great many mourn the date as also the anniversary of India's Partition, which caused the holocaust of a million people and forcibly displaced an estimated 10 million across both the borders of Punjab and Bengal. There are those ultra-liberal Utopians who wish Partition had never happened, while the more ardent nationalists decry the sundering of *Akhand Bharat* (Undivided India). Then there are those who are realists; this group realises that Partition was inevitable. However, if one were to say that it was desirable, one would be hauled over the coals for political blasphemy.

Let us for a moment assume a hypothetical alternate scenario of there being no Jinnah or his campaign for a separate state for Muslims. Had the British left without overseeing Partition, Hindu-Muslim antagonism would have inevitably escalated and finally erupted into civil war. Such a civil war would have converted India into a hotbed of unending sectarian strife. Assuming that the British had left India in 1947 without Partition, it would be naive of us to believe that the Muslim League would have simply given up on its struggle for a separate state for the *qaum*. After all, what was Direct Action Day in 1946—upon Jinnah's clarion call—all about?

Had Partition not happened, an undivided India would today comprise over 40 per cent Muslims. Any honest observer would know how tactical voting would have consistently produced a Muslim prime minister. Before long, the sovereignty of the people of India would have shifted on to the lap of Allah the merciful, the foremost precondition of an Islamic state. This is not mere conjecture; doubting Thomases should read Pakistan's Constitutions. As to what this would have meant for the subcontinent's Hindus, one need look no further than next door. For that matter, Pakistan itself, a state conceived as a theocracy, is a failed state.

India would today be a democracy only in name—if at all. Not a prospect Indians would have looked forward to. The energies of Hindus would have been consumed in trying to survive with a hostile population of over 50 crores. As a consequence, India, far from the incipient major power that it has become today, capable of reaching and exploring outer space and writing software code for the world's corporations, would have become the biggest battleground of medieval religious strife. Hindus who harbour any doubts on this score need look no further than the fate that befell Yugoslavia after the end of the Cold War.

US in Black and White

IT IS DIFFICULT to imagine a brown or a white man doing for me what a black classmate did at college in 1956. I scored 63 per cent in the subject of Modern Europe and 55 per cent in Modern India, a total of 400 marks in the final BA examination of the University of Bombay in 1956. Incidentally, 60 per cent marks, which are deemed a first class, were quite creditable in those days. I achieved all this by merely reading my African friend's notes twice; I had hardly done any preparation in those subjects for my exams and had to borrow his notes which he generously lent me.

We had been friends, classmates and hostel mates for four years. His name was Robinson Martin Muyunda Musole. He was from Northern Rhodesia, now Zambia and had come to Elphinstone College, Bombay (now Mumbai) on a bursary of

Rs 200 or more per month. This was India's way of making friends with Africa's young. My friend went on to become the head of all education in Zambia, immediately north of Zimbabwe. Someone else called Omolo from Kenya eventually became his country's Attorney General. In our hostel as well as college there were boys from East Africa. They were older than their classmates, better read and knew more English.

Musole became a close friend. In the first two months, he complained to me that Indians harboured racial prejudice. In all these two months not a single girl had spoken to him. Was that not prejudice? He asked me on the way to college from the hostel, a distance of some two km. I answered his query in the afternoon in his hostel room since it had to be in private. My advice was he take his several pairs of cotton shirts and trousers and give them to the *dhobi* for washing. I also suggested he shower twice a day for the next three months with sandalwood soap. At home, he was used to wearing woollen trousers and a good quality English shirt, which he seldom sent for washing. This had turned out to be a problem not only with girls but also with the boys who had to interact with Musole.

In a month's time, with the new clothes, he had many more friends, both boys and girls. In two or three months' time, he had learnt to sing Hindi film songs, particularly one from Dev Anand's movie *Patita*. Musole had a melodious voice and was a hit with the girls at picnics. Thereafter, he had no social problems that I came to know of. We remained in fairly frequent contact but less than at the start of his Mumbai sojourn. Evidently, he had made many more friends. I was happy for him.

The moral of this experience was that when people of two races come in contact for the first time, some organised introduction for a few days should take place. This is necessary so that the visitors come to know the culture of the people they are visiting. A great deal of prejudice arises from lack of familiarity, which, if it takes long to come about, could lead to misunderstandings. If that persists, it is bound to grow into prejudice which could endure indefinitely, often across generations as has happened across the world. In the USA it is explicable because unfortunately the Blacks there came as slaves.

By the same token, cannot the reverse be true? In recorded history, we find that wealth has commanded respect. This phenomenon began with the advent of feudalism and has continued with capitalism. Communism was a direct assault on wealth, whether it was called means of production, landed property or by any other name. The wealthy were delighted with the demise of communism although the rich did not wisely celebrate the defeat lest it provoke a backlash. To think of an Indian example, though quite unrelated, the educated among Dalits generally support capitalism. Those of them who become rich command respect, which this writer has seen for himself. Even successful politicians, ministers et al are saluted, as was (former) President Barack Obama.

To begin with, the commercially rich, the industrialists or the traders did not evoke an equal status. The landowners were the aristocracy while the commercials were the business folk; there were the *boxwallas*, who in turn called the shopkeepers 'shoppies'. Respectable clubs would not normally admit such people, however rich, merely because they lived off shops or stores. If they applied for membership, they were blackballed, a name that possibly takes after the lingo of a game. This distinction between the wealthy without a business and rich without an industry still exists. The former curiously evokes more deference. Nevertheless, over a period of time,

Goddess Lakshmi is worshipped most by those who empathise with wealth. When feudalism and land ownership fell, the industrialist took its place.

For capitalism, there is no better society or country than the USA. The solution, therefore, lies in letting capitalist enterprises flourish on parallel lines. In any case, most businesses begin as family enterprises. Let them grow larger and larger; if necessary, along the lines of colour. If blacks wish to invest in white companies, let them do so as they do now. If whites find some black enterprise(s) profitable or lucrative, they should be free to invest in them. If they are reluctant to invest in such companies, so be it. If there are any behavioural problems of the blacks, let the whites come out openly and speak about them. This would provoke a debate and possibly bring about a substantial solution.

Neither the blacks nor whites are so shy as to not express their feelings frankly. Robert Mugabe, the late President of Zimbabwe said: "Racism will never end as long as white cars are still using black tyres. Racism will never end if people still use black to symbolise bad luck and white for peace. Racism will never end if people still wear white clothes to weddings and black clothes to funerals. Racism will never end as long as those who don't pay their bills are blacklisted and not white-listed. Even when playing snooker, you haven't won until you've sunk the black ball, and the white ball must remain on the table! But I don't care; as long as I'm still using white toilet paper to wipe my black ass, I'm happy".

Evidently, the colour black is objectionable in some countries; in such societies, its use in this sense could be abolished and replaced by another colour of mutually popular choice, for the simple reason that no community considers black to be either an auspicious or benign colour.

Normally, when a compromise is reached, one side or the other, or both, have to give up something. Whereas in this suggestion, there is no giving up by anyone on either side; it is what may be popularly called a "win-win situation". There is, therefore, no need to resort to any form of radicalism, whether political, ideological or religious. The central spine of American culture happens to be Christianity. For the blacks, therefore, it is best to stick to the central theme, rather than display the slightest sign of revolt.

Outsourcing—an Old Practice

FOR SOME YEARS, responsible opinions have been expressed that as a part of India's modernisation, worker laws need to be reformed. The opinions, however, have remained as good intentions well preserved. Meanwhile, economic growth has been slower and the outcry for more jobs is getting louder. The problem with the current industrial laws is yet undiagnosed and, therefore, a cure has not been found. The writer has, in his endeavour, gone back two centuries. What was it then and what it could be now?

Outsourcing of work by business, industry, et al was first witnessed two centuries ago. The need then was of British traders who knew their trade but were utterly alien to conditions in Bengal. S Das Gupta in his book *Echoes from old Calcutta* wrote:

> Banyan is a person who either acts for himself or as the substitute of some great black merchants with whom the English gentlemen are generally to transact all their business. He is interpreter, head bookkeeper, head secretary, head broker, the supplier of cash, and cash-keeper, and in general also secret-keeper. He puts in the under-clerks, the porter or doorkeeper, stewards, bearers of the silver, slaves, running footmen, torch and french light-carriers, palanquin-bearers, and all the long tribe of under-servants, for whose honesty he is deemed answerable, and he conducts all the trade of his master, to whom, unless pretty well acquainted with the country languages, it is difficult for any of the natives to obtain access. In short, he possesses singly many more powers over his master than can be assumed by any young spendthrifts, steward, moneylender, and mistresses all together.

The cause originated in the demands justified by the Industrial Disputes Act, 1946, which was incidentally like a parting gift to India before the British rulers departed for good. They meant well, especially when one thinks of the arbitrary, exploitative behavior of the employers in the early decades of the twentieth century and before. No one could have foreseen the effects of the legislation in the context of militant trade unions of the later decades. The militancy was not confined to Kerala and West Bengal but also prevailed in Maharashtra, as well as Haryana. The north was marked by muscle whereas the Mumbai region produced more interesting varieties including monetary militancy.

For example, a union was led by one RJ Mehta which lent money sufficient to keep the body and soul together of the worker members through the entire strike period. The workers, therefore, did not get impatient to settle with the employers. The loans were recovered with reasonable interest from the hefty increments Mehta squeezed from the management. Plus, he took from the workers a large share of the increments for the first one year of the agreement. In Mehta-led agitations and strikes, no violence took place! The tactics, including the ultimate personal violence, adopted by Datta Samant, a medical doctor, were again unique. The managements had mostly no answer but to surrender to the demands. Some of the enterprises collapsed after a time, so vexatious became the workers' pay and perks.

To amend substantially the ID Act at this stage would be difficult; the trade unions have by now too many vested interests in the legislation. Even the affected workers would not like any undue changes. It is, therefore, best to frame a new law as an alternative to the ID Act. New projects could easily opt for the new law under which the workers are employed. For the established industries, let them carry on under the ID Act. When their three, four or five contracts between the workers and employers expire, let the managements tempt or persuade the unions to sign the new contracts under the new Act. If not, carry on and renew their agreements under the old law.

From the workers' viewpoint, under the old or current law, the statutory or retiring dues are not adequately protected, especially if the employer company were to close down prematurely. They may or may not get their gratuity, leave encashment or even the full provident fund. Under the new bankruptcy laws that have been recently brought, there may be quite a few quick and urgent closures. The first step the alternative legislation should take is to plug this probable misfortune. The safest way to do so would be to give say a separate bank draft of 25 per cent of the monthly salary or wages every month. This draft should not be cashable for five years so that the employee cannot spend it immediately but willy-nilly has to preserve it as a genuine saving.

The second feature of the new law should be that the wage be gross or all-inclusive and, therefore, without odds and ends in perquisites. This would enhance the worker's savings paid as part of the 25 per cent draft. Thirdly, the appointment would be terminable with a month's notice. This would encourage entrepreneurs to promote worker-intensive projects, and also seasonal businesses without fear of being burdened with employees without work to allot subsequently. This fear keeps many a medium or bigger size employment-intensive project from seeing the light of day. This is sad especially for the lesser-educated or trained men and women. These are just the young people who need a break, an opportunity to learn a vocation on the job and prove that they can also 'do it'.

This writer is an example; he had a total of only eight years' formal education. Had he not got an early break, he might have had to live with being a clerk, or even a peon. There are today too many jobs being advertised, especially by public sector corporations, which however insist on the applicants being graduates. Yet, there can be a good number of class X and XII pass boys and girls who may prove brighter than graduates. We also need to remember that there are a large number of schools and colleges which need to come up in the standard of education that they need to impart. The candidates consequently also vary a great deal in the quality of what they know although they hold respectable degree cards. The new law we make should take into account all these sociological realities and not just confine itself to the terms of employment.

The old law is not merely obsolete but also indulgent. For example, it permitted trade unions to pressurise managements to employ more workers than necessary. One way was to assign designations to them. Say, a gum carrier in a cigarette factory. His department would require a refill every 45 minutes, a piece of work which would take him say ten minutes at a time, eleven times in the course of an eight-hour shift. Thus the gum carrier had say two hours' work. The other six hours, he sat around without work. Another example: to unload a wagon of tobacco, there were gangs of 14 workers. In case two or three of the particular gang members were absent, the manager could not borrow substitutes from the next gang. He had to take on temporary workers while the next six gangs merely sat and twiddled their thumbs. Quite extraordinary as it may sound, most factory managers had to collect, by deducting from the wages, the trade union subscription of every worker. The intention was to bind every worker to the union which, in turn, often agitated against the company. The arrangement is called 'check off'. So incongruous can be the results of a law when it is cunningly twisted.

Origins of Prejudice

THE ORIGIN OF the prejudice against black complexion cannot be ancient. Krishna, the eighth incarnation of Vishnu, had a dark complexion and is invariably portrayed in blue. Another version of Krishna, and a popular one, is Srinathji whose famous temple is situated at Nathdwara, north of the Chittor Fort in Rajasthan. He is always portrayed in black. A few years ago, Prof SR Rao discovered the original city of Dwarka established by Krishna which had, in an earthquake, sunk to the bottom of the sea. Most of the retrieved artefacts of Dwarka have been preserved in the Museum of Oceanography in Goa. Prof Rao considered Krishna to be contemporaneous with the Harappan (Indus Valley) civilization. This means that the acceptance of the dark complexion is not unduly old.

Prejudice against the blacks in America began as recently

as the 18th century when the slave trade from Africa began. Until then, it was not unusual to have blacks as prominent characters in European literature. Othello, the hero of the great Shakespearean tragedy *Othello* is an example. The question arises whether such prejudices are related to power. In India, we have people of virtually all complexions and there is no social prejudice against any of them, although when choosing a bride there may well be a preference for the fair and lovely girl.

This is all very surprising when one thinks of the four year bloody American Civil War fought between the northern Unionists and the southern Confederates. While most white people on both sides of the divide reconciled themselves to the new post-Civil War unity, a fringe of the blacks could not march lockstep with the rest of the nation.

Much earlier than the American Civil War, sincere efforts were made by several white leaders to either abolish slavery or make it softer. The slave trade was dominated by British slave traders. Yet, the leader of the Abolitionists was a gentleman from Hull in Yorkshire, England. He was William Wilberforce, a Cambridge graduate born of well-to-do parents, and of liberal sentiments. He leaned towards evangelism for quite a while in his life, and at other times, towards Methodism. It is possible that religious sentiments had their influence on Wilberforce's views. He was a Member of Parliament for a good ten years.

Wilberforce had another great advantage in the pursuit of his cause; he was friendly with William Pitt the Younger. Pitt became the prime minister at the age of twenty-four and continued to remain the head of government continuously for twenty-two years. Essentially liberal in his outlook, Pitt supported, as far as politically possible, the cause of abolition of slavery.

The slaves, thus, had the sympathy and help of two powerful Englishmen. Yet, the vested interests must have been so deep-rooted that the acquisition of slaves on the west coast of Africa, called the Horn of Africa, continued. It was not until a Bill called the Slave Trade Act of 1807 by the British parliament that serious political steps began being taken towards ending this inhuman activity.

For the practice of slavery to be abolished though, it took several more years till the passage of the Slavery Abolition Act in 1833, again by the British Parliament. This abolished slavery in large parts of the British Empire. The 1833 Act was essentially an expansion of the jurisdiction of the 1807 Slave Trade Act. However, no matter what the British Parliament did, vested interests located outside the British Isles continued with their profit-making. African slaves were captured inland by Arab slave traders and then handed over to British traders. The hapless Africans were then transported in ships that had very little space and no toilets. Imagine sailing across the Atlantic with no toilet at all in the hold. How suffocating and horrible such a voyage must have been? Many of the slaves so herded across the ocean died during the voyage, which also shows how cheaply they had been acquired. In other words, the traders who had got hold of them could afford to lose a substantial number.

The accounts of these atrocities, both narrated and read, prompted any number of sympathisers to plead for the slaves. Their names included such distinguished individuals as William Ewart Gladstone—Prime Minister of Britain from 1868 to 1894 and many others.

However, the role of the American Civil War (1861-65) is seminal in ending the practice of slavery in the Western world. It was a war that threatened to undo the United States of America itself. Had the USA not remained a single country after its Civil War, it is a matter of conjecture as to what the fate of Western civilization would have been. One thing is certain though, a divided USA would have been a great threat to this civilization. Imagine what would have happened as a result of German aggression and imperial ambitions in Europe, resulting in both the World Wars, had there been no undivided USA to come to the aid of and preserve the liberal Western civilization. What if there had been no USA to stand up to the (now deceased) Soviet Union, an equally dangerous foe?

As an aside, my own familial experience with Africans might be instructive in bringing into focus how prejudices or preconceived notions might hamper mutual understanding among communities. One of my nieces is married into a Christian Nigerian family. I attended the wedding in New Jersey. I discovered to my surprise that the Nigerians were different; they were better educated and culturally more polished. Since the family was Christian, the wedding was held in a church. About one-third of the population of Nigeria follows Jesus Christ and is concentrated in the south-east of the country known as Biafra. According to their custom, speeches were made by relatives of the bride and bridegroom. Overall, their side made impressive speeches and altogether appeared to be better, at least by Western standards.

It has been a happy marriage, and their values appear to be like those of a joint family, not very different from an Indian one. My niece's husband was an FRCS from London but this qualification was inadequate for him to practice in the USA; he, therefore, took up another surgery course good enough for his new country. Ten years later, the new surgeon heads three hospitals in Pennsylvania and is flourishing. The couple have three intelligent daughters who all wish to study at Ivy League universities like Harvard and Princeton. On balance, these West Africans appeared a lot superior to their East African cousins. The point I am making is how different the people in different parts of the world are than we presume.

Another niece is married into a family which hails from Jamaica and is settled in Toronto, Canada. They are educated and are all professionals. They are well-read and betray no complexes. They are quite indifferent to the colour of their skin. Two of the ladies are almost as white as Europeans, while two others are black. The men are of mixed colour, the kind that are described as 'mulatto' in South Africa. In short, our observation was that they could not care less about their complexions. The marriage has been a happy one and her husband is quite popular amongst all our relatives.

What is striking about both these families is that they had no interest in talking about their problems, either racial or national. For example, the Jamaican did not talk about their difficulties in their native country, which had been the reason for their migration to Canada. Despite my probing, none of the Nigerians seemed prepared to discuss the civil war of 1967 in their country between the southern Biafrans and the northern Nigerians, and its accompanying slaughter. Their uniform answer was that all that was a long time ago. For us Indians, there is a lesson to learn. When we go overseas, we should avoid discussing our communal, linguistic or casteist disputes with foreigners.

Religion and Geopolitics

A TRUER UNDERSTANDING of Hindutva would be useful. Then such unfortunate incidents as Advocate Rajiv Dhawan tearing up a map of old Ram Lalla mandir, in the presence of the senior judges of the Supreme Court, might not occur. The advocate might have meant it as his tribute to Indian secularism but it has turned out to be an affront to an idea that is perhaps the only hope for world peace. Most people cannot spontaneously see the connection nor has anyone yet made an effort to point it out to them.

The Abrahamic religions assert that theirs is the only God whether Jehovah, Jesus (son of God) or Allah. If a follower has any doubt, he is not a true believer. By the same token, all who do not believe in Jehovah are gentiles, those not believing in Christ, infidels, in Allah, kafirs. These are what the deductive section of logic would call given premises. What flows from them would be the corollaries, which in the light of the premises, flow flawlessly. For example, if one accepts that Allah is the only God and his Prophet is Muhammad, the corollaries of Islam are literally flawless and utterly logical.

Judaism does not favour conversion but Christianity and Islam do believe in proselytisation and expanding the number of Christians and Muslims around the world. Expansion, domination and possibly war are the corollaries. Since Independence, India has had to fight several wars with Pakistan, including one on Bangladeshi soil. Although in 1971, we helped it to get free, subsequently there have been tensions, including their soldiers beheading our jawans, with many infiltrators and some terrorists crossing over. The behaviour of Islamabad towards India and cross-border infiltrations by thousands is a continuing saga.

On the other hand, neither Nepal nor Sri Lanka or Myanmar have been troublesome on the Indian borders. They happen to have Hinduness at the core and have not aligned themselves with Pakistani activity. The number of Christians in India is fewer than Muslims, but in any case, they haven't involved themselves with any separate political activity. There is no Christian political party.

The question is: what is so distinctive about Hinduness that it can emerge as a fountain of peace. There is no assertion about God, unlike in the Abrahamic faiths. From Vedic times, the emphasis of Sanatana dharma is on karma. Deeds lead to destiny; karmas are eventually rewarded or punished by *bhagya* was a concept that satisfied the upper, educated sections of society. The common folk needed something more tangible.

The concept of *swami* and *das* subsequently, treated as

God and worshipper, was introduced by the *bhakti* saints—Chaitanya Mahaprabhu, Tulsidas, Surdas, Eknath, Tukaram, etc. These saints helped to attract the attention of common folk towards Hinduness. Thus, they did not go over to Islam. Incidentally, the status of *swami* or God was given not to God but his avatars (incarnations). Ramachandra was considered the seventh avatar of Vishnu, while Krishna the eighth and Buddha the ninth. Similarly, there are objects of worship by the hundreds like the cow, the banyan tree and the river. These were treated as objects of veneration with the social objective of preserving and protecting them. Divinity could certainly not have been awarded to such a large number.

Unlike the Abrahamic faiths, Hinduness is not the result of a deductive premise initiated by the concept of God or Allah. If there is logic in Hinduness, it is attached to the reality on the ground and argued upwards to a conclusion. This is nearer the inductive wing of the science of logic. To illustrate further, suppose four Hindus from four different corners of India met and each one claimed to have seen a different-coloured rose. Eventually they would agree to disagree and conclude that what each had seen must be true of their respective regions. On the other hand, if these four persons were Abrahamic they would part in disagreement.

The Hadith exhorts men to marry women who are fecund so that one day the community would be more numerous than any other on earth. At the same time, family planning by artificial means is not allowed. Due to high infant mortality, the Hindu practice in the olden days was no different. However, there were no restrictions, as a result of which reforms were easy enough to frame and enforce. For example, family planning amongst Hindus faces no resistance.

In contrast to the will to dominate experienced by the Abrahamic faiths, Hinduness has opted for self-actualization of the individual. The motivation is more individual and much less collective. The idea is for each person to tune his karma to how well he wants to do in life. It is possible that many might not be consciously ambitious and live life as it comes. This probably is the factor which makes many a Westerner conclude that a Hindu is a fatalist. What is necessary to know is that life is a journey of continuity as the soul moves from one body to another upon every death. Early *mukti* or salvation is the reward for exceptional karma.

To emphasise the point, the aspirational Hindu strives to ensure excellence of his karma and thus fully self-actualises himself or herself in an activity in line with aptitude. A collective effort has almost always received a backseat in the Hindu ethos. At the best or worst of times, there has been hardly any Indian aggrandising effort. Imperialism beyond the borders of India has been, as it were, an anathema to Indian rulers. The Cholas did travel far and wide across South East Asia, but their thrust appears to have been culture and trade, rather than governance.

Coming to the question of peace in the world, it can be achieved only by nations that do not aspire to either conquer or dominate other nations. The European nations like Spain, Portugal, the Netherlands, Britain and France needed to be richer, and went to conquer colonies. Despite being rich in resources, the New World is unable to restrain itself from trying to dominate other countries.

A thermonuclear world which has several countries with atomic arsenals, forces us to ensure that no war breaks out. In 1945, two small atom bombs were dropped on Hiroshima and Nagasaki. They were sufficient to shake-up the world, the proof of which is that since then no atomic weapon has been used. Today, the known arsenals are estimated to be large enough to destroy the earth three times over. This is only to emphasise how ensuring positive peace is a desperate need.

There is no ethos, idea or ideology, which can enable such a peace, other than self-actualising Hinduness.

China's Compulsions

THE COMING MONTHS are the time to tell Beijing that the occasion to settle our mutual issues and disputes is now. Those pending since our independence and your People's revolution cannot go on forever. The lingering disputes must be ended or else, sooner or later, the American alliance will expand. India has been non-aligned and its rulers would prefer to continue that way. It would be a sad day if one Asian country drives another Asian nation into the arms of the West. It is for Beijing to balance the cultural, economic and strategic damage of an Asian split or the blossom of Asian unity. This is the time to act.

The external affairs situation is gearing itself into a remarkable opportunity for New Delhi to regain what we lost in 1962 and before. It is as if many a planet is positioning itself to assist India. It began with Chinese ruler Xi Jinping becoming highly ambitious, apparently wanting to make his Middle Kingdom the powerful pivot of the earth. Like Napoleon Bonaparte in 1804, Xi has crowned himself Emperor for life, although the world has changed a great deal over the last two centuries. Today, any number of his colleagues would resent such a royal elevation, and implicitly compel Xi Jinping to prove himself a great man every week.

The USA had an unusually bold president. President Donald Trump had been waging a cold war with Beijing for quite a while. It has become colder of late and is likely to freeze further. He demonstrated in Texas earlier this year how much he likes Prime Minister Narendra Modi. Lately, he along with his Secretary of State Pompeo has openly supported India in the context of Chinese border intrusions, although their main concern is Taiwan, a democratic island-country off the southeast coast of China. It is an independent country but Beijing claims that China, Taiwan and Hong Kong-Macao are one country but three systems. The USA has a defence treaty with Taiwan and cannot possibly allow the island-country to be grabbed by China. Nevertheless, it is a matter of 'do or die' prestige issue for Beijing, especially in Asia. It will, therefore, be interesting to see how the issue will unfold.

According to its president, the USA is likely to jettison the North Atlantic Treaty Organization (NATO). Think of it, it was an alliance to combat an invasion of Western Europe by the Soviet Union. By 1991 the Soviet Union had broken up. After that what is the rationale for NATO? Who should it defend, and against whom? In any case, this should mainly be the responsibility of Western Europe, not the USA. If this were to happen, the US military budget would have a lot of money and troops to spare for Asia. Half the American troops stationed in Germany are already being transferred to Asia.

After World War II ended in 1945, Germany and Japan were asked by the USA and allies to hold back any military operations. They were forbidden from letting their forces leave the shores of their countries for any military engagement. In fact, for the first five years after WWII, these countries were not to have any military at all. They were to be protected by the USA, with or without NATO. Germany remained conservative, saved money and produced its economic miracle. Japan was militarily a little more ambitious and began developing its navy and air force and strengthening its army, even though slowly. In these seventy years, it has quietly modernised its navy and air force, has built a helicopter-carrier and also makes modern submarines.

The then Prime Minister, Shinzō Abe, has worked hard to amend the Constitution and Japan can now send troops overseas. The more China developed, the greater grew the Japanese intent to be militarily stronger; so also is the case with India over the last six years. Similarly, the people of Taiwan have been alerted especially after the trouble began in Hong Kong. Until the Xi Jinping regime passed a law that anyone arrested for wrongdoing in Hong Kong could be extradited to mainland China for being tried, these smaller places were relaxed.

This new Chinese law has made Hong Kongers rightly feel wronged. They feel it is a violation of Beijing's commitment of 1997, when the British left, of "one country two systems" whereby the mainland would not interfere in Hong Kong. Popular protest in Hong Kong spilled over to the streets where even American flags were flown, provoking great anger in Beijing. These continual agitations have further alerted the Taiwanese and in a recent election, a lady, Tsai Ing Wen, became the island nation's president. Tsai is very committed to complete independence which infuriates Beijing no end. The USA is defending Taiwan's freedom to demonstrate its seriousness. Very recently, a Secretary of the Trump government has visited Taipei as a show of support. India under Prime Minister Modi has appointed an envoy to Taiwan, following the Ladakh clashes.

More distant countries, whether in Europe or South America, have become resentful of China; they suspect that the Corona virus began in Wuhan, a province of China, and yet China did not alert them. The international wind is blowing against the yellow giant. The Islamic countries may not speak up but are upset at how Beijing is treating Muslims in its country, especially those living in Xinjiang, which was once an independent East Turkestan.

Sino-Japanese relations have an uneven history. For example, Manchuria was a colonial province of Japan between 1932 and 1945. As a result of World War II, it was ceded to China. Over the many decades, especially after its naval victory over Russia in 1905, Japan has considered the Pacific Ocean more as its own than anyone else's. Lately China has been spreading its wings over the South China Sea, which is objected to by several powers including Japan as well as the USA. Beijing has built an island in its midst provoking Australia, India, Japan and the USA, who have deployed their navies to do naval exercises in the seas. The Senkaku Islands are a group of uninhabited islands. Apart from a 1945 to 1972 period of administration by the United States as part of the Ryukyu Islands, the archipelago has been controlled by Japan since 1895. The People's Republic of China (PRC) started talking of the question of sovereignty over the islands in the latter half of 1970 when evidence relating to the existence of oil reserves surfaced.

Additionally, after claiming large portions of the South China Sea as well as Mt Everest, two Chinese websites have been claiming that central Asian countries like Kyrgystan and Kazakhstan have been parts of China with the latter even eager to return to China. According to the latest Chinese territorial claims on others' territories, under the Khan dynasty, 510,000 square kilometers of Kyrgystan, which means the entire country, was part of Chinese lands but the Russian Empire took over the territory.

It is well-known that China is over-populated and land-hungry. In the bargain the People's Liberation Army had tried to cross the Ussuri river and cross into the Russian territory in 1969. The vast area of Russian Asia has comparatively few people and is, therefore, a perpetual temptation for the Chinese to occupy. Beijing has few friends for fear of what it is and what it could desire. North Korea and Pakistan are the only obviously perceptible allies.

UAE and Israel Rapprochement

THE ESTABLISHMENT of diplomatic relations by the United Arab Emirates (UAE) with the Jewish state of Israel must rank as not merely a huge surprise but also an incipient remaking of West Asian politics and possibly the global order as well. The United Arab Emirates opening its embassy in Jerusalem will be looked at, particularly by Islamic countries, as a stunning development. Jerusalem is regarded by Muslims as the third holiest city of Islam after Mecca and Medina. They believe that Prophet Muhammad started from the spot where the Al-Aqsa mosque currently stands in Jerusalem, on his celestial horse Barak to ascend to heaven to meet Allah and return.

A sacred city and also a contested one, officially being recognised as the capital of a Jewish state, and obtaining diplomatic affirmation from another Muslim state is not exactly pleasing news for many faithful. Lesser would have been the consternation had this mutual recognition of diplomatic status been centered on Tel Aviv, Israel's former capital or any other city. Jerusalem happens to be a holy place for Christians as well; Jesus Christ is believed to have been born in Bethlehem only a few kilometers away. He lived, preached and worked in the area around Jerusalem. The Calvary Hill on which the Son of God is supposed to have been crucified is located in the holy city, along with the Church of Nativity, where he was buried.

While this action of the UAE—an amalgamation of seven principalities led by Abu Dhabi—has raised eyebrows galore and more questions, it goes without saying that such an action could not have been unilateral; there must be a substantial Islamic consensus behind it. While on one hand the UAE's West Asian neighbours—Iran, Turkey, Syria, Iraq, China, its sidekick Pakistan and possibly Russia will most likely carry antipathy to the UAE's action, it is unlikely the rest of the world would lose much sleep over it. It certainly is a split bigger than ever before among the Islamic countries.

Readers might wonder at the reason as well as the implication of this Judeo-Muslim 'entente', so to say. Except for those countries named above, Saudi Arabia, the guardian of Mecca and Medina, is the leader of the Islamic world, and must have cleared the UAE action before it was taken, even if not overtly so. This also means that this is the beginning of a cataclysm in Islam, which has until now been comparatively a united world community or *quam*, headed by a religious-cum-temporal head called the Caliph.

There have been changes, about-turns and diplomatic cataclysms before. In 1972, US President Nixon, accompanied by the guru of world affairs Henry Kissinger, visited Mao

Zedong, then the undisputed leader of Communist China. The USA was known to be dead set against Communism as well as the countries that followed the red ideology. Moreover, Red China was known to be a 'brother' of the Soviet Union, the first communist state as well as the other pole in the Cold War, the first pole being the US. America's Western allies were certainly taken aback; Japan, Taiwan and South Korea being so near the yellow giant were stunned for quite a while.

This UAE-Israel agreement evokes the question about the feasibility and desirability of separating politics and statecraft from religion. Islam is one faith which includes every aspect of life, not merely the relationship between humans and the divine. In this light, this latest turn in the Middle East is a cataclysm. Islam and Judaism are theologically similar; the former has borrowed substantially from the latter and yet there has been hatred between the two. Its political shade exacerbated after Britain declared in 1911 that the Jews would get their holy land in Palestine. Until then, the Jews residing in that country were unwelcome to the Muslims, but not hated to the extent they later began to be.

There have been several wars between the Arab states and Israel after the latter was founded in 1948, with Arabs being worsted each time. The eastern half of Jerusalem was taken away from the Muslims in the war of 1973. Now the whole city is integrated and has been made the capital of Israel. Recognition of Jerusalem as the capital of the Jewish state has been, religiously speaking, possibly the touchiest issue with the Muslim world and Islamic states. But with the UAE now agreeing to open full-fledged diplomatic relations with Israel without making any noise about Jerusalem, with barely a whisper from much of the Arab world, it does appear that there are winds of change blowing that transcend political realignment.

The UAE is currently ruled by a courageous soldier-prince, Sheikh Mohammad bin Zayed Al Nahyan—whom Prime Minister Narendra Modi had invited as the chief guest for India's 68th Republic Day in 2017. He has proved his diplomatic vision by striking this deal to normalise relations with Israel. In return, Israeli Prime Minister Benjamin Netanyahu—another close friend of Modi—has agreed to suspend plans to annex parts of the West Bank. It also provides an opportunity for Israel and the Palestinians to renew negotiations to end their conflict. Bahrain has welcomed the deal and is expected to be the next Arab state to reach public rapprochement with Israel. Oman and Morocco are interested as well. Not surprisingly, President Trump of the USA had wholeheartedly welcomed this rapprochement between Israel and the UAE; this deal is a triumph for his Middle East doctrine. It has breathed new life into his "Peace to Prosperity" plan, engineered by his adviser and son-in-law, Jared Kushner. This also indicates that the Palestinian cause is of little concern to the UAE and increasingly other Arab states, and is no longer an obstacle to peace between Israel and them.

What might have caused this change of thinking, if not of heart, among Arab rulers with regard to Israel? For one, the Arab states, and Saudi Arabia in particular, are possibly beginning to realise that Israel does not threaten them in any manner. The real threat looming in their part of the world is now Iran, whose apocalyptic visions of another Islamic revolution, combined with its messianic drive to acquire nuclear weapons, have the propensity of unleashing an Armageddon in West Asia and the rest of the world.

But there are deeper developments at play in the West Asian part of the world that have dictated this slow but discernible change of heart among the Arab countries vis-à-vis Israel. The Arab Spring, which kicked off in 2011 and was instrumental in bringing down the Hosni Mubarak regime in Egypt, was a limited measure of the slow but definite churn going on in the Islamic world and West Asia in particular. The current Iranian regime is constantly in the news for its defiance of the West over its nuclear programme and links with terrorist groups; less reported is the fact that for the past one year, Iran's citizens have been up in arms against their regime. Significantly, anti-government protesters in the streets of Tehran chant "America is not our enemy". These Iranian demonstrators are said to carefully avoid walking on US and Israeli flags painted on the street outside one university. The reason for these protests is the slow but growing realisation among Iranians that their country's medieval regime, run by the theocratic mullahs, threatens to make Iran an international rogue state.

A 2012 WIN/Gallup International poll found that 5 per cent of Saudi citizens—more than a million people—self-identified as "convinced atheists". Approximately 19 per cent of Saudis—almost six million people—think of themselves as "not a religious person". This phenomenon has visited other Islamic countries with harsh anti-apostasy regimes like Pakistan, Iran and Sudan, which have seen desertions from the faith.

This phenomenon points to a reality we usually do not hear about—many young Muslims are suffering from a crisis of faith. It is being abandoned by moderate Muslims, mostly young men and women, ill at ease with growing extremism in their communities. Noted Turkish-American economist and Professor of Economics and Political Science, Timur Kuran in his book *The Long Divergence: How Islamic Law Held Back the Middle East* (2011) summarised the institutional roots of the Middle East's economic stagnation even as the rest of the world, particularly the West raced ahead. Quite possibly, many in the West Asian part of the world are waking up to the fact that shutting the door on *ijtehad* (reasoning) and enforcing *taqlid* (orthodoxy) is now costing them a lot. While it might have been dictated by the circumstances that prevailed when their faith was founded, the 21st and coming centuries of unimaginable scientific advances and technological revolutions leave no space for such exclusivism. Hopefully, this realisation might turn out to be a lasting one.

Whither Communist Parties?

WITH THE BREAK-UP of the Soviet Union in 1991, the skies of all communist states in the world were overtaken by dark clouds. Before long, most of these states lost their red governments. Over the last three decades the era of Karl Marx has passed, although the red political parties in some counties are still flickering, for example in India. In China, the entire party has not only survived, it also monopolises the political life of the huge country, although the Marxist ideology has been consigned to history. The Communist Party of China lives on in all its glory; its only missing feature being the ideology of Marx and Mao. North Korea is similar, although the leadership of the party is a family dynasty.

Let us assume that sooner or later, communism could revive in Europe or come up say, in South America, or anywhere else due to widespread unemployment. There is not even a remote possibility of it reviving, not to talk of succeeding in India. The irremovable obstacle in the path of any movement that promises equality is Hinduism. Its core belief in karma enables the poor person to reconcile to the fact that unless one's karma improves, there is little chance of his or her fate improving. Any other promise would be like a balm that may relieve the pain without curing the disease.

Let us go back to the early years of Indian independence; there were too many poor people in most parts of the country. Much of the poverty was unbearable to see. Yet, none of the Marxist parties could impact the many elections held throughout the country, except for Kerala and Bengal. The people of these two states were well endowed with brains and thinking which spared comparatively less energy for physical work.

The Marxist promise of "from each according to his ability to each according to his needs" militates against the Hindu belief in "no *bhagya* (fate) without karma". In other words, the Indian electorate was never an attractive playing field for the communist politician. With Marxism itself having been now discounted, obviously the red politicians must search for an alternative path. Which one can it be?

A party grows in order to either serve a collective cause or redress a chronic grievance. In India, there is no shortage of grievances. The biggest segment of people who have the most grievances would be the womenfolk. The petition before Supreme Court, which transferred it to Parliament, was over instant *triple talaq*. The real triple divorce, namely, *talaq-e-biddat,* which takes over three months to complete is still alive, but it is still entirely discretionary in the hands of the woman's husband. Another Damocles' Sword hanging over the womenfolk in India is polygamy. Another grievance, as well as a cause, would be family planning, which can attract the female vote. Yet, it is virtually a neglected cause since 1977, when Indira Gandhi lost the general election because of *nasbandi* (vasectomy) being in its manifesto.

A greater national issue can be a Sino-Indian settlement over territory and borders. With their communist credentials, India's communists should be the best placed to negotiate with the Communist Party of China. The CPI (M) would be ideally placed as they sympathised with China in 1962 and split from the main Communist Party in 1964 on the issue. The CPI at the time was in sympathy with the Soviet Union, which nevertheless had called the Chinese 'brothers' vis-à-vis the Indians being just 'friends'. Additionally, there is the Revolutionary Socialist Party (RSP), the devotees of Leon Trotsky's Permanent Revolution, plus the Socialist Unity Centre which owes its origins to the Communist Party of East Germany.

A particular strength of the communists has been that many party members are educated. Could they not promote their electoral prospects by running schools and colleges? They could also do other forms of social service like hospitals, dispensaries and nursing homes.

The late Chief Minister of Tamil Nadu, MG Ramachandran, was the first major mover in this regard, introducing the mid-day meal in schools. His successor J Jayalalitha arranged for idlis to be made available at Rs 5 a plate to the public. The Shiv Sena in Bombay, years ago, won acclaim for opening *jhunka-bhakar* stalls that provided both livelihood to many youngsters as well as affordable meals to a large section of the state's working population.

The communist parties have cadres, including permanent

ones that could help in organising these welfare schemes. On the other hand, they could take a leaf out of the book of their erstwhile communist associates or comrades from East Europe, who did not hesitate to jettison communism and become social democrats. After the fall of the Berlin Wall in 1989 and the collapse of both communism and their overlord the Soviet Union in 1991, the communists of Eastern Europe undertook a variety of reform processes.

The collapse of communism posed a fundamental challenge to the ruling communist parties of East Central Europe. After 1989-1990, they were removed from their international imperial hierarchy with Moscow at its centre. The Warsaw Pact, the military alliance that was the opposite number of the West's NATO, also ended with the collapse of the Soviet Union. East Europe's communists now stood rejected as the roguish elements of an ideology and worldview that was delegitimised. Worse, they were no longer in power, as they were dislodged from the pinnacle of authoritarian regimes. Without regimes to rule or states to govern, the leadership of the former ruling communist parties had to find a new purpose, or what one might call a new strategic vision, to survive in the new world of post-communism.

The reform process of former East European communists and their parties was done in accordance with both changed political realities as well as the nature of the transition that their societies had undergone. They, therefore, took up different agendas in their respective national situations. Subsequently, former east European communists adopted different attitudes towards issues of European integration. The Polish, Czech, Slovak and East German successor parties all underwent different experiences in their respective polities and societies.

But they all changed. As communist parties they voted themselves out of existence and declared themselves to be social democrats or any other name, in keeping with the changed circumstances. By the time the early 1990s arrived, former communist political parties were already active and playing leading roles in social, economic and political developments of East and Central Europe. However, India's communist parties, leaders and their ideological supporters paid scant attention to these developments.

In India, words like welfare and *kalyan* would be appropriate to rename the parties, if necessary. Since health, education and other welfare are insufficient in India, this approach of a political party could succeed. "Workers of the world unite" is a slogan that has been out of date for over a century. One thing is certain: there is no future for communists in India unless they change. The communist parties with their structure, organisation and their entire cadre would go waste.

Krishna Janmabhoomi

IN ORDER TO enjoy peace as well as prosperity, India has to improve the relations between Hindus and Muslims. That was one of the premier messages of the last two Lok Sabha elections, namely 2014 and 2019. Instead of taking note of this noble sentiment, Muslim and secular leaders as well as most of the media blamed the so-called Hindu Right with mistreating the Muslims, especially after Akhlaq Khan was killed in Dadri (UP) on suspicion of cow slaughtering. Thereafter, there were several incidents of attacks on cowherds because they were transporting cows allegedly for slaughter. A few intellectuals and writers were killed in Karnataka and Maharashtra. The Congress-ruled governments could not apprehend the criminals nor pinpoint the likely cause for the crimes. The total number of those killed in all these crimes did not exceed twenty-five.

It is alleged there has been one riot (in Delhi) in the course of the years since May 2014. Contrast this scene with all the years since 1947.

If one looks through the history of Hindu-Muslim riots in the British rule and until 2014, it is not easy to find another period of six or seven years when non-violence has prevailed across the country. Yet, there have been more complaints of insecurity by Muslims as well as secular lobbies. A top film actor's family went to the extent of saying that in the midst of this insecurity there was no future for them in India. The repeated expressions of anxiety added up to so much provocation that on the morrow of his becoming Prime Minister, Imran Khan advised India to learn from Pakistan how to treat its minorities. A German associate, who is familiar with India, happened to be in Delhi at the time. His comment on this whole situation was that Hindus were more to blame than anyone else. We were surprised at this statement as he knew that most of the time Hindus were at the receiving end.

The German, Erich Baumgartner, went on to say, "You Hindus are many more in number, richer, more educated, and yet you complain you are at the receiving end. Why? What is lacking in you? Prima facie nothing. Look back at your record even after the Great Mughals' rule ended after Aurangzeb in 1707. There is nothing on record that the Hindu chieftains tried to replace the Badshahs, Sultans or Nawabs anywhere. When the Marathas overran Delhi, they broke to pieces the throne of Emperor Shah Alam I, and made him a tax or *chauth* payer. He was not displaced. In fact, decades later, his successor after his defeat was granted a pension. Is there a single comparable such action in any history?"

A young history lecturer was around when we talking.

He interjected to assert that Hindus are so broad-minded that they did not do anything to the Muslims as revenge. It was the British East India Company that dispossessed the Sultans in India. Robert Clive defeated Nawab Siraj-ud-Daulah at Plassey in 1757 and pursued him thereafter to kill him at Rajmalal in Bihar. Thus eastern India fell to the Company. In the south, Lord Wellesley took on Tipu Sultan at Seringapatam in 1799 and saw the end of him. Lord Dalhousie dismissed Nawab Wajid Ali Shah of Awadh in 1856 and imprisoned him. Thus ended the Muslim rule and the British Empire was established.

The German guest turned to me and asked, "Are you satisfied with my remarks about who is to blame? Even in the 20th century, the Muslim League was formed first in 1906. The Hindu Mahasabha came in 1915 while the RSS was established in the year 1925. By signing the Lucknow Pact, Mr Tilak conceded separate electorates, job reservations and weighted representations. Mr Jinnah was delighted. Even greater delight was experienced by him when Mr Gandhi called for Quit India and Congress leaders disappeared into jails for four years. Meanwhile, Jinnah's League had a field day running ministries and building political bases. Pakistan was won in the jails of India. You Hindus are more philosophical than political. Don't run away from this reality. If you want to see ancient India, go to Mathura."

Hearing the name of this district, the Professor at once suggested reading the Memoir of FS Growse of the Bengal Civil Service, 1882 (IAS of the 1960s). He was for years the Magistrate of the district. Its most famous temple—that dedicated to Kesava Deva (Krishna)—was destroyed in 1669, the eleventh year of the reign of the iconoclast Aurangzeb who descended on Mathura. The temple specially marked out for destruction was one built as recently as the reign of Jahangir, at a cost of thirty-three lakhs, by Bir Singh Deva, a Bundela Rajput chief of Orchha. Beyond all doubt this was the last of the famous shrines of Kesava Deva. The mosque (*idgah*) erected on its ruins is a building of little architectural value. Mahmud Ghazni was, however, the first iconoclast to vandalise Mathura. That was in 1017 AD about which Growse wrote: 'If any one wished to construct a building equal to it, he would not be able to do so without expending a hundred million dinars, and the work would occupy two hundred years, even though the most able and experienced workmen were employed'.

Among the spoils are said to have been five great idols of pure gold with eyes of rubies and adornments of other precious stones, together with a vast number of smaller silver images, which, when broken up, formed a load for more than a hundred camels. Today Balkrishna is worshipped in a little room like a servant quarter attached to the back of the *idgah*. Pathos can be experienced by any visitor, whether a devotee or otherwise.

To go back to Aurangzeb, over two centuries after the desecration of the temple, Growse wrote that: 'Of all the sacred places in India, none enjoys a greater popularity than the capital of Braj, the holy city of Mathura. For nine months in the year, festival follows upon festival in rapid succession and the *ghats* and temples are daily thronged with new troops of wayworn pilgrims. So great is the sanctity of the spot that its panegyrists do not hesitate to declare that a single day spent at Mathura is more meritorious than a lifetime passed at Banaras. All this is due to the fact of it being the birthplace of the demigod Krishna'.

Entitlement Complex Causes Unhappiness

EVEN AFTER SOME 800 years of association, Hindus and Muslims are unable to communicate clearly with one another. Is the lacuna because of insufficient contact? Or is it because the two communities function on the basis of two distant presumptions rigidly cherished? It would be interesting to delve into the latter and discover the presumptions, if any.

The author had a teacher for conversational Urdu for eight long years. As it happened, the relationship also grew into a friendship, spontaneously enabling free and frank conversations. Agha Iqbal Mirza was a graduate of what was then the Delhi College, who dressed in a suit and on most days wore a bow tie. Unfortunately, early in his life he tried to do business again and again, but failed. Once when asked, he boldly declared that he was a Muslim first, a Muslim second and everything else later, but not a pro-Pakistani. He was a Mughal, whose ancestors had come from Central Asia; he should not be confused with an Afghan Pathan, who calls himself a Khan. His family name was Mirza; it could also have been Baig.

As the relationship grew, the writer once asked him why he suffered from an entitlement complex; his reply was that his attitude was based on what he considered were his rights. Being a Mughal, he knew that his clansmen had ruled India from 1526 AD to 1758 AD, a good 250 years. Babar had captured his Delhi throne by defeating Ibrahim Lodi, a Muslim. The same throne was lost to the East India Company and not to a Hindu. "We, therefore, do not look upon the Hindus as enemies," he said. Bahadur Shah Zafar, the last poet-emperor, was captured and exiled to Rangoon (now called Yangon) in Myanmar or Burma.

When asked: What about the Hindus? Mirza's response was: "What about them? The Mughals built so many forts and monuments and most of the time, ruled the country efficiently. Incidentally, the architecture is still earning India tourist money. Look at all that Emperor Akbar did to encourage agriculture and collect fair revenue from it". But when Mirza was questioned as to why Muslim rulers did not develop any modern industry, or do anything in that direction, his reply was that for one thing the Mughal rule ended too early for an industrial revolution. He added that we must remember that fundamentally Islam believes that what Allah the merciful provides, Muslims should be satisfied with. For them, he went on, it is advisable to gracefully accept what Allah gives. Flapping about money is like complaining to the Almighty that He is not giving enough. This could imply that He is not being fair, or not doing justice. How could one ever allege that about God? We work as best as we can and thereafter leave it to Him.

When this writer expressed his belief that a person's duty was to put in his best; we call it karma and hope that it would be rewarded commensurately with *bhagya* (fate or fortune), Mirza intervened with vehemence to say I was wrong. "Your Gita," he said, "exhorts you to work but without attachment to the fruit of your work. Is that not true? How is your theology superior?" The writer quietly asked: "Isn't there a difference between accepting what one gets and trying hard to get what one wants? If you do not get it, the message for the Hindu is not to break his head over it." Mirza chose not to pursue this argument any further. Instead, he diverted to history and how Muslims have always been given a raw deal.

What right had Robert Clive to come to Murshidabad, displace and kill Siraj-ud-Daulah? By and large, the nawabs in Bengal had been providing good and fair governance. To the British, they had provided a large part of Calcutta and several commercial special rights. "I am sure," Mirza asserted, "that the big Hindu businessmen secretly helped the British. Incidentally, Bengal was the richest *part* of India. This was a big blow to Islam in India. From rulers, the Muslims in the region overnight became subjects." Mirza quoted Rahimtullah Sayani, a business magnate of Bombay and President of the Congress, as saying, "How a stroke of ill-luck has brought Muslims down to the level of their Hindu countrymen."

Soon hereafter was imposed English education, which the Hindus took to happily because they had become used to learning the languages of their rulers. This turned the tables with Hindus gradually becoming superior and ousting the Muslims from their positions. The good teacher continued, "What else can you expect but the Two-Nation Theory and eventually Pakistan? In an undivided India, all or most Muslims would have sunk to the bottom of the sea. Are you not seeing my fate? Above everything else, my education and all, I am the proud grandson of someone who was the *kotwal* of Delhi."

Notwithstanding the illegitimate British invasion of India, Sir Syed Ahmad Khan of Aligarh fame advised all Muslims that they should support the British. They should not agitate as the Congresswallahs were going to do. "Do not join that Hindu party" was his exhortation. "If we remain faithful to the British," said Sir Syed, "if and when they leave India, they could well leave the government of India to Muslims, if for no other reason than the fact that they had dispossessed us of most of the country."

To come back to Agha Iqbal Mirza—when the writer asked him why he did not opt for Pakistan, he gave a complicated reply. "Firstly, Pakistan was not created to make people like me homeless. It was meant to be a homeland for those Muslims who insisted on living in a Dar-al-Islam. That there is such a state on the subcontinent is a matter of great satisfaction for me and others like me. Secondly, if there be riotous violence against us in India, we would have a protector of ultimate appeal. Thirdly, to actually move to Karachi or Lahore would be very difficult. For example, I have no capital and that is why I am working for you for Rs 700 a month. I would have to find money enough to travel to Pakistan and enough to survive there for a few months before I get settled. Would the job or occupation there be to my liking?"

He went on to say, "the way you have asked me this question, it seems as if my right to be in Calcutta or Delhi at the stroke of midnight of 14/15 August 1947 has expired. That might be European thinking but not Islamic. Land or *dharti* is not the anchor of our lives, certainly not collective life. We are not *vatanparast* (worshipper of one's country)." He continued, "Where one stays is incidental. In whom I believe, who I worship is all important. Allah is the epicenter of Islam. Neither Muslims in India nor those in Pakistan were particularly disturbed by the secession of Bangladesh. By the same token, whether I live here or in Bangladesh or Pakistan, or for that matter in Arabia makes no difference to Allah the merciful."

There must be any number of co-religionists who must feel the same way. If so, why is there so much ado about the Citizenship Amendment Act (CAA)? Infiltration, immigration or emigration do not count in the Islamic contexts. All land is Allah's; all the three Constitutions so far passed in Pakistan begin by asserting that sovereignty over the entire universe belongs to Almighty Allah alone.

Poet Mohammed Iqbal, whom we applaud frequently, wrote a second *tarana* (song) after *Saare Jahan*. In it he asserted that not only the whole of India but also China and Arabia belong to Allah. Muslims should live in this world like fish live in the ocean, without boundaries, unlike caged animals in the zoo.

Religion vs Culture

GOVERNOR ARIF MOHAMMAD Khan hit the nail on the head when he said that some people make the mistake of equating culture with religion. The reason is that they look at things from Western or Semitic frame of reference. The subject of Logic has two broad sections, namely, Deductive and Inductive. The former section begins reasoning with a clear-cut premise without assigning any explanation. For example, Judaism asserts that Jehovah is God, Moses the Prophet and the *Torah* the scripture. What follows are the logical corollaries of this premise, all of which the believer is expected to accept while on his/her journey to heaven which ends on doomsday.

Allah the merciful is the God of all those who happen to be Muslims. Muhammad is the last Prophet and the *Quran* the final message for all those who consider Abraham as the first

Prophet of all. The Quran is supplemented by the Hadith or Traditions and the Sunnah which records the lessons of the Prophet's life. Between these scriptures, the momin or the faithful Muslim gets a complete prescription for how to live life individually as well as collectively. There is, as it were, no need to look left or right. The Islamic scriptures lay out all possible dos and don'ts, the halals and harams about which the believer does not need to ponder or hesitate. The logic of the religion flows like a river as if it were a necklace of perfect pearls.

Christianity preceded Islam, and among the Abrahamic religions has on paper more followers than either Islam or Judaism. Islam acknowledges Jesus but as a prophet and not as a son of God. Moreover, governance is covered by the religion whereas the Bible assigns politics to Caesar as the emperor was called in those days. As a result, separating the Church from the State was possible when the Reformation came in the 16th century. However, the religion of Christ has grown into many denominations, each having a somewhat different theological view. By contrast, Islam stopped *ijtihad* or reinterpretation of theology which was reflected in the Sunni (about 90 per cent Muslims) attitude to the Ram mandir at Ayodhya.

At stake for the Indian people is the perpetual Hindu-Muslim equation. There are differing views on the subject. MA Jinnah is believed to have said that Pakistan was born the day the first Hindu was converted to Islam. In contrast, MK Gandhi had told British Prime Minister Ramsay MacDonald in London in 1931 that Hindu-Muslim riots are coeval with British rule. The rule ended seventy-three years ago but riots still go on; remember the Partition was meant to be a solution to the problem. In that context, Jinnah's separatism did take the pressure of Islam off the other communities. He, however, had in mind a complete exchange of populations as designed by the League of Nations and implemented in 1923 between Greece and Turkey and between Bulgaria and Turkey. Dr BR Ambedkar endorsed this proposal but the Congress leaders paid no attention to the idea.

Going back to Logic, the Deductive section goes clearly up and down—a given premise followed by its corollaries and reasoning. The Abrahamic faiths follow this approach. Inductive Logic is the reverse; there is no given premise. The facts, data and sentiments are gathered from the ground, the people and the reasoning moves upwards until a conclusion is arrived at. This is free reasoning; nothing is given. Hinduism, Indic faith or what is often referred to as Sanatan Dharma or Eternal Faith or Virtue follows the Inductive path, which would explain the multiplicity of Hindu denominations? One of the few common factors that runs through all of them is karma leading to fate. This equation is as near as faith can get close to Science or Physics; for every action, there is an equal and opposite reaction.

This fundamental difference between the Deductive and Inductive approaches is clear and sharp. The former insists on its viewpoint and does not concede the opposite contention; hence fights and wars have been frequent. For the Deductive to be at peace with the Inductive is more difficult. This is the Hindu-Muslim syndrome. While the sultans and nawabs ruled there was no way the Hindus could riot. This violent civil phenomenon began after these rulers were brought down from their thrones. Remember that the dethroning work was performed by the British East India Company. Robert Clive vanquished Nawab Siraj-ud-Daulah in 1757. Lord Wellesley saw the conclusive end of Tipu Sultan in 1799 while Lord Dalhousie pushed out Nawab

Wajid Ali Shah for the Company to take over Awadh in 1856. These were three corners of India; the western fourth comprising Rajasthan and Gujarat remained in the hands mostly of rajas. Gwalior, Indore, Kolhapur and others also survived as princely states until Independence in 1947.

Strangely, there have not been Hindu-Christian riots although there have been incidents of Muslims killing Christians, especially in Pakistan. What the circumstance are in that country, we do not know. We do know that we need domestic peace and the high priests of Islam need to explain to their followers that there is no alternative but to coexist with the Hindus. How to do so is not difficult; they merely have to follow the Christian example.

The Mistakes Super Commissars Make

PARADOXICALLY, PRESIDENT XI Jinping appears to have been inspired by the old imperial tradition that 'everything under the heavens belongs to the emperor'. He has got himself elected emperor by a communist central committee. Josef Stalin, Russian dictator (1924-53), similarly dreamt super dreams. Before World War II, Russia was a normal European power. There was no superpower in Europe. It was the American influence on the continent, during and after the war, that gave rise to this new geopolitical concept. Moreover, many Russians believed that they had primarily won the war because they reached Berlin first; so perhaps did Stalin. Thereafter, presumptuously, Moscow postured as a superpower equal to the USA. America had the atom bomb and, therefore, the Soviet Union had to have one, no matter the cost. By 1952, the Pentagon had exploded a thermonuclear device. Stalin was impatient, and regardless of the cost proportionate to the Soviet economy, had a thermonuclear bomb ready in 1953. That was not really beating the USA and hence, the Sputnik, the world's first artificial earth satellite was floated in October 1957. Here, the USA appeared overtaken in the space race.

Stalin died in 1953, but his spirit of superpowerdom, no matter the cost, carried on, to the extent that the First Secretary, Nikita Khrushchev, thumped his shoe on the table at the United Nations. He also told the USA and implicitly the entire capitalist world that, 'We shall bury you'. No matter who the First Secretary or Prime Minister was, the intoxication carried on merrily until Mikhail Gorbachev became the First Secretary. He immediately knew that his country was well past bankruptcy and called for *perestroika* (reconstruction) and *glasnost* (openness). But hardly anyone could realise that it was US President Ronald Reagan and his programme of 'Star Wars' that had finished the Soviet economy. It was a competition in escalation of arms, which the Soviets could not afford, and they fell by the wayside. To try and make it stand up, India's then Prime Minister PV Narasimha Rao doled out $1 billion to Moscow when Boris Yeltsin was President. Meanwhile, the 16 Soviet Republics that made up the Union broke up.

The empire the Tsars had so assiduously built over two centuries crashed in 1990-91. It took at least three decades until after the World War II, before the USA devised a clear-cut, simple strategy to defeat the Soviet Union. That began when President Ronald Reagan came to power in 1981 and condemned the Soviet Union as an 'evil empire'. He decided on an arms race to test how far the Soviets could sustain such a race. They could not build anything similar to what the Americans had envisaged, i.e., platforms in the skies to fire lasers at and destroy incoming ballistic missiles. The Soviet rulers could apparently not understand what was going on. All they knew was that they were short of every kind of necessity—food, consumer goods and industrial manufactures of sophistication. Yet, they did not cut down on their military budget. In fact, President Gorbachev of the USSR reiterated his predecessors' policy by stating that his country would 'match the Star Wars build-up of the USA'. Evidently, he was oblivious of the economic situation his country was in. There was no comparison between the economic strengths of the two powers and the inevitable crash of the USSR happened.

Nevertheless, it was also President Gorbachev, the last of the Soviet Union's First Secretaries who was the first one to see the rot within his country's system. He embarked on *perestroika*, which meant reconstruction. Well-wishers of Russia would have wished that he had stopped at *perestroika* and not coupled his reform programme with *glasnost*, or openness or democracy. These two reforms together led to chaos rather than any improvement. The contrast can be seen in China under Deng Xiaoping, wherein he confined his country's reforms to *perestroika*. Of course, Deng's words were: 'The colour of the cat does not matter so long as it catches mice'. To this day, over thirty years later, there is no real *glasnost* in China. There has been *perestroika* all the way but no freedom or democracy. Those classes who have enriched China and themselves through these reforms obviously feel powerful. The question is: will they remain subservient in a communist regime, or seek a democratic vote before long?

Communist China has pursued the same autocratic path as has been its tradition for the last twenty-two centuries, as was the Russian, from time immemorial. The Soviet regime was called a 'dictatorship of the people'; before 1917, it was the imperial rule of the Tsars. The modern rulers probably presumed that the old blood runs in the veins of the modern youth, whether rich or poor. In reality, the soil is ideal for a dictatorship so long as the society is feudal. The time the Soviet Union turned into an industrial autocracy, the inefficiencies began to show up. The Soviet rulers did not have the vision to detect this decline. The Second World War, to an extent, enthused the workers and concealed the deficiencies. In this context, the worst enemy is the absence of democracy. The rulers do not obtain any feedback from their people. Those who provide such feedback do so through the screen of terror.

The other factor is that autocracy, whether Russian, Soviet or Chinese, acts as a perpetual inebriant and keeps the rulers out of contact with their people. In the bargain, they should have plenty of time to think about governance, although they miss out on what their people want. This disconnect is an eternal fault of a dictatorship. The Commissars have suffered from it; the Chinese less and the Russians more, perhaps because they have learnt a lesson from the Soviets. Another fault of autocracy is the immediate feeling of power in the ruler. The wiser person restrains himself. While retiring, Deng Xiaoping had advised his successors to 'hide their strength and bide their time'. Three of his successors followed this advice; namely, Zhao Ziyang, Jiang Zemin and Hu Jintao. They took care not to annoy the USA. China traded prolifically with the West and deposited dollars with Washington. All was hunky dory.

President Xi Jinping, however, is given to ambition and has had himself declared emperor and thus made it clear that he is recalling the entire past imperial era of his country. The Chinese call themselves the 'Middle Kingdom' and their emperor has represented the heaven on earth. Earlier American presidents, confident in the American supremacy, did not take much notice of all this. President Trump, however, was a businessman by vocation and recently, the world has been ravaged by the Covid-19 virus, which began from the city of Wuhan in China. Business is an exchange of goods or services for money and not for anything else, including diplomacy or flattery. China, however, recently veered from the path of business to that of overt power. In the process, it has very few friends other than North Korea and Pakistan. This may not be the fault of the communist ideology because history has seen any number of dictators drunk with power embarking upon disproportionate campaigns and leading their countries to ruin.

GLOBAL

Laws, Jobs and Reality

MY RIGHT TO work is fundamental although the Constitution does not say so. But then should governments, whether the Centre or the State, put obstacles in the path of whatever employment I can get? A recent stipulation is that my potential employer must pay me a minimum of Rs 15,000 per month. Unfortunately, I lost my father early and did not get an opportunity to study beyond class V. My mother asked me to do some work and bring home at least Rs 50 every evening. I did succeed for a few days, until the police threatened my employer with punishment for employing child labour. I was therefore out and back home to the distress of my mother. As an adult I was eligible for a regular job but no one I approached was prepared to pay me more than Rs 8,000 with the promise that I take a cheque for Rs 15,000 and return to the company

Rs 7,000 in cash. The question was: do I stoop to this corrupt practice or sit at home?

Come election time, and young people are promised jobs. When I was getting a job, I could not accept it, legally speaking. Why are our political rulers so unaware of the gulf between laws made by themselves and the economic realities prevailing in the territories they rule? My boss, for whom I was working as a domestic help in exchange of food, clothes and an allowance, had tried to explain to me. According to him, this contradiction from which I was suffering and many others too, was a Russian baggage brought to India by Jawaharlal Nehru. Communist Russia, then known as the Soviet Union, guaranteed employment to everyone. This was a wonderful measure, very humane. Unfortunately, it was one of the causes that led to the Soviet Union's bankruptcy and eventual collapse.

Nehru was a socialist, so he did not go the whole hog in communism. His Constitution does not guarantee any employment to anyone. On the other hand, nor did his government try to understand capitalism or how social democracy functioned in Europe. More unfortunately, Nehru's successors, no matter which party they belonged to, did not bother either to understand the syndrome and young people like me became the casualties of our leaders' negligence. Capitalist USA continually carries a percentage of unemployment, as do the social democracies of Europe. These countries have a variety of unemployment doles. On the other hand, India has welfare promises and legislations galore, without any thought being given to their implementation.

Over the last several years, the people have become quite conscious of the need for development. There is also frequent talk in cities of India becoming a superpower. We have abandoned socialism but are yet to think through an alternative. In any case, because of the size of the country and its many people, it is difficult to discover a viable alternative. A bigger complication is the variation in economic development from region to region; there are varying levels of poverty and prosperity. Why not then give all the people full freedom to choose a job, an employer and a level of pay and perks which he can afford and the employee can accept, with no controls whatsoever? This absolute freedom would offer a fighting chance that we may, before too long, reach full or near-full employment.

There was a time when an unemployed person could live off his family, which in turn, depended on farming its land. But now, with increased population and the reducing size of most farms, this alternative for a man without a job or income is no longer there; so it would be difficult to survive. Therefore, some income is a must. A low wage is better than no wage. The flip side of this situation should be an encouragement to entrepreneurs. Demand for handmade goods, especially in the affluent world, is believed to be limitless.

A Morgan Stanley report of a few years ago had stated that India's labour laws force firms to remain small, employ fewer workers, or to use capital-intensive technology. No wonder the share of India's manufacturing sector in GDP terms is one of the lowest among emerging markets. Our track record in creating productive jobs has been poor. How can there be any productive job growth if the country's labour market is shackled with regulations made 60 or 70 years ago? Another factor so far overlooked is that work itself is a training as well as experience. Even if a youngster has missed sufficient schooling, his early start in a job can offset the disadvantage to a significant extent. On the other hand, if a young man or woman has to be without work for several years they would lose self-confidence, learn little and lack experience, which is a springboard for building a career, however humble. An idle mind is a devil's workshop, but the imposition of a minimum wage ignores this old wisdom. In assuring one person a comfortable wage, it ruins up to nine potential careers. These nine include those who remain jobless merely because the minimum wage stifles the economy's growth.

Laws and regulations like the minimum wage, say Rs 15,000 per month, touch only the economy's organised sector. In India, this covers only 16 per cent of the worker population. The remaining 84 per cent are in the unorganised sector and do not benefit from government stipulations. On this basis alone, there is a strong case for lifting all wage stipulations. They serve only the electoral blandishments of a political party. Few political leaders realise the deathly effects of the minimum wage policy on the employment prospects of their young constituents.

Labour Law is a concurrent subject under the Indian Constitution. Thus, both the central and state governments have the right to formulate laws on the subject, which means multiplicity of laws, at times with overlapping jurisdictions. For example, there are 44 central laws and about 160 state laws on the issue of labour (source: ILO, 2013). Most are archaic, dating to the pre-independence era. There is an urgent need to overhaul these laws to attune them to present realities. There are multiple laws governing a single area. For instance, there are 19 laws governing conditions of work and industrial relations, 14 laws on social security and labour welfare, etc.

Freeing the employment market should have been one

of the obvious answers to India's jobs problem—and a workable as well as imperative one. But neither politicians nor policymakers seem to even want to venture near this solution. In India since 1991, we have talked, written and debated *ad lib* on liberalisation, globalisation and the ease of doing business. However, not a drop of ink has been spilled on completely freeing the employment market. Discussions on new or alternative labour laws do take place; so do talks on minimum wages. Do we not realise that such tinkering of this nature would take the economy nowhere? From time to time, the Delhi government raises minimum wages to seek applause. Some labour or trade union leaders do lend their palms for clapping but that would be about all. But such moves do not increase employment, if anything, paradoxically, they bring down wages.

The Industrial Disputes Act has been the parent of Indian thinking on virtually all employment, except for the uppermost layer of officers and executives. When the Act was passed, the government intended it essentially for workers. Because of the low salaries prevailing then, clerical staff got included. In the absence of any other guidelines, the situation has degenerated to the extent that any employee can file a suit in a labour court. As a result, every responsible employer thinks not twice but thrice before making appointments at Class II, III or IV levels. As far as the number of jobs is concerned, it is these categories that are critical. Employers, up to a point, take shelter in outsourcing. However, such proxy appointments can hardly be a help in generating jobs on a national scale.

If one wants to see glaring examples of what damage the Industrial Disputes Act and its corollaries have done in India, one may visit West Bengal. This state, which was once India's leading industrial province, became a graveyard of industries. Kerala is another state which is also a cemetery of industries, albeit a smaller one, because the ID Act-inspired trade unionism stopped the state's economic growth early in its tracks. In the heyday of monopolies and restrictive trade practices, a majority of large business houses were headquartered in Kolkata. The ID Act-bred trade unionism effectively chased them out. It is, therefore, time that India chases out the ID Act.

Unions, prima facie, are to protect and promote the welfare of their member workers. As it happens, most unions are affiliated to one political party or the other. Their leaders have their political ambitions. In the bargain, the priority of their loyalty may be the party. Moreover, fundamentally, the strength of a trade union lies in the number of its members; their welfare is a lower priority. Further, the concept of the worker's union is traced to the desire for revolution; aiding and abetting to bring down bourgeois institutions.

A paradox of the Indian scenario is its large population. Also the demographic dividend on the one hand, and minimum wages declared by state governments plus the laws and labour courts being prejudiced against employers on the other. Another paradox is the national outcry for more jobs. None of the points we have made so far help achieve greater employment. If anything, they actually shrink the prospects for employment.

It is, therefore, advisable to scrap all these laws, including the Industrial Disputes Act. In their place, a worker-contract bill should be passed, which would be between an employer and an employee, in accordance with their mutually agreed wishes, including the salary/wage. The only universal condition should be that 25 per cent of this salary should be handed over as a draft of a public sector bank, payable exactly five years later. These drafts, month by month, would be the employee's post-employment benefits. This is to assure him/her that even if the employer closes down, the benefits are safe. Otherwise, there should be total freedom, which would enable numerous projects, especially labour-intensive, to mushroom and bloom.

All in all, the appeal of this submission is for looking at Indian conditions through Indian eyes and not through a socialist heart. Most worker rules have a Marxist flavour if not an origin, including the British practices until the years of Margaret Thatcher. Many of India's laws are borrowed from British traditions.

A Necessary Evil

THE MENTION OR even the thought of nuclear weapons sends jitters down the spines of almost everyone. The reaction is universally one of horror and rejection. On the morrow of the Balakot raid by the IAF Mirage warplanes, many people the writer interacted with reminded him that Pakistan has the atom bomb. The refrain was: would Pakistan's General Bajwa use it in retaliation to India's destruction of the Jaish terror factories in Balakot? Some exclaimed: what a curse the bomb is for mankind! Others said: the nuclear bomb will one day bring doomsday upon humanity, even if God fails to do so! However, in this cacophony of views and sound-bites, what is strange is that this writer did not hear any cries of pessimism from a Muslim mouth. Is this optimism what the faith inspires? Or is it fatalism? *Allah Tala ki jo marzi hogi*. (Whatever god wills)

One thing is certain, though. Those who indulge in wholesale condemnation of nuclear arms are either ignorant or prejudiced, or both. Do they not see and recognise that the world has not seen a fighting/killing World War since 1945? World War II, on the other hand, followed WWI within just twenty-one years. Between these two cataclysms, seventy-four million human lives were consumed. Then one must not also forget the Cold War wherein the major portion of the world was involved. The Soviet Union, one of the protagonist blocs of the Cold War, lost the conflict and broke up into sixteen countries; not just that, an entire ideology—Communism—met its demise across the world. The 43 year (1948 to 1991) engagement, therefore, can be called World War III although there was no overt fighting as neither superpower fired a gun nor killed each other's soldiers. Yet, a two-century-old Czarist Empire, which had morphed into the Soviet Union, was torn asunder. In the process, the greatest challenge to the capitalist ideology was put to sleep for ever.

The credit for a nuclear holocaust not happening ought to go not only to the presence of nuclear weapons, but equally to the fact that the US Air Force actually dropped two of them over Hiroshima and Nagasaki in August 1945. But for this atomic bombing, no one would have seen or visualised what monstrous damage a bomb, not much larger than a volleyball in size was capable of inflicting. How two cities and most of their people and buildings, all went up in smoke in less than an hour. Had such a mega holocaust not been witnessed by the human eye, some misguided soul either in the Kremlin or in the Pentagon might have just touched a button and simply unleashed a thermonuclear colossus over civilization. Even doomsday might have looked child's play by comparison.

The likelihood of a naive finger pressing a nuclear button is not all that difficult to imagine, particularly so, if one harks back to Napoleon Bonaparte ordering his Grand Army to march to Moscow, knowing fully well that winter visits the year like a turning wheel. The resulting fate of the Grand Army as well as the eventual destiny of L'Emperor at Waterloo are well known. Did the next would-be conqueror pick up any lesson from Napoleon's denouement? Not the least. Adolf Hitler—and it is only fair to assume here that the Fuhrer must have been acquainted with French history—embarked upon his venture so close to his heart, Operation Barbarossa, in June 1941. All he achieved was to convert his hitherto triumph in Western Europe into the ghastly tragedy of Stalingrad. The turning wheel of the Russian winter would forgive no one. Yet, the intoxicated conqueror never restrains himself and Hitler proved he was no exception to this rule. It is by no means inconceivable that a similar villain might have one day gotten his hands on the nuclear button. But for the holocausts of Hiroshima and Nagasaki, the unthinkable might actually have happened.

By 1948, the USA would have manufactured a good number of atom bombs. This was the year when the Soviet Union made the city of Berlin out of bounds by land. The Soviet blockade of Berlin was sufficient provocation for a proud American president to threaten to drop an atom bomb in order to relieve the Soviet ring around Berlin. It did not happen; evidently, the USA did not wish to repeat the sin of Hiroshima. The world, however, found itself staring at the nuclear precipice in 1962. Under its leader Nikita Khrushchev, the Soviet Union tried to pull a fast one over its rival. It tried to surreptitiously install nuclear missiles in Cuba pointed northwards at the USA. Washington caught on to the conspiracy as well as the danger; its southern state of Florida is just a stone's throw away from Cuba. The US prevented the Soviet ships bringing in the warheads but only on the threat of doing another Nagasaki. In the eventuality, neither side ventured to risk a nuclear clash, although it was the Soviet Union which had to blink first.

Nine years later, the shadow of a nuclear Armageddon loomed again, this time over our own subcontinent. In 1971, during the Indo-Pak war over Bangladesh, there arose another threat of a nuclear clash. The USA dispatched a part of its Seventh Fleet led by the aircraft carrier *USS Enterprise* to the Bay of Bengal in the month of December that year, to bolster the beleaguered Pakistani forces, which were at the receiving end of a rapidly advancing Indian army. To cover the Indian army and to thwart any American bullying, the Soviet Union sent its nuclear submarines to stalk the Seventh Fleet and particularly the *Enterprise*. Although it appeared a nuclear showdown would occur in our backyard, both sides hung on to their restraint; neither side fired a bullet.

While the sands of time ran on until 1971 and no nuclear device was used, quite a few other countries joined the USA and USSR in going nuclear. Britain became the third nuclear power in 1955, followed by France, which created its own nuclear force called "Force de Frappe". The nuclear club was looked upon as an exclusive arena and the insiders were determined to keep it that way. That was not to last for long; China went nuclear in 1964. India shed its pacifist inhibition ten years later in 1974. Pakistan, whose scientist AQ Khan smuggled out nuclear technology from the Netherlands, joined the club after India tested a second time in 1998.

So far, members of the nuclear club have accepted that such weapons are a symbol of international status as well as defence against nuclear blackmail but not weapons of utility. An American writer has described the possession of nuclear arsenals as achieving a mutual balance of terror. In short, possession of such arms has become an invaluable defence so long as a country doesn't use it. Iraq, Libya and Serbia were invaded and their governments overthrown; they were helpless in the absence of a nuclear deterrent. It is not surprising, therefore, that North Korea and Iran, learning from this experience, have pursued a deterrent.

On Conflict or Culture

HOW RIGHT HAS American political scientist, Prof Samuel Huntington, been proved! Broadly speaking, since the 1972 Munich Olympic Games, when a dozen Israeli athletes were massacred by Islamists, members of the Islamic culture have been at war through terrorism against other cultures. No doubt, until very recently those of the Western culture have been patient. The massacre of 51 Muslim worshippers in Christchurch, New Zealand, in March 2019 was the first instance of determined retaliation against Islamist terrorism in various parts of the world.

Another phenomenon which however, has gone uncommented upon is another face of class conflict. Yes, communism expired soon after the fall of the Berlin Wall in 1989, followed by the break-up of the Soviet Union into 16 republics. That trade unions had begun to weaken and union terror had begun to die was not clearly noted. In a broader historical perspective, it is as if class conflict departed and was replaced by culture clash. In the bargain, we are witnessing one phase of history being replaced by another. What follows is a brief examination of how classes came into being and how they clashed, and how their conflict began to end. The question arises: is the world becoming classless or are classes reconciling themselves to coexistence? This was once theorised as class collaboration or fascism.

Adam and Eve did not come into being as members of a class. Social organisation began as clans and tribes living in rural areas whether forests or otherwise. Whatever land and property that developed, belonged to the community, neither to a family nor an individual. There was no farming or regular agriculture; people ate what they could hunt, cut or pluck. Land as such had no particular value in the people's minds. That consciousness came when farming began and crops provided food and materials like, for example, cotton.

The ownership of land grew into a temptation; it became a major measure of wealth. The more the land owned, the greater the landlord. The greater the land and the farms, the more the workers required to till. The captive workers became the serfs. That is how feudalism came into being; the landlords grew into the pillars of the monarchs. The monarchies expanded into empires. The serfs turned into soldiers and the various landlords provided the hierarchy of knights or officers in times of war. The feudal structures or networks served the monarchies, big or small, in the time of peace as well as when wars took place. Thus a feudal society developed its own classes; the royalty, the aristocracy of landlords, knights and squires, and the farm workers, peasants with a little land and finally serfs with virtually no land.

With the advent of capitalism based on manufacture which expanded more and more with the growth of the industrial revolution, the economic importance of land-based feudalism became smaller. With manufacturing or industrial growth, towns and cities became bigger and bigger. The share of this sector in the total economic value became larger; the proportionate value of farm produce became comparatively smaller than before. But the class mentality that the owner is superior and the worker is inferior persisted. The owner took it for granted that it was his privilege to extract as much work and production as possible for the least possible payment to the worker.

This extraction of more work for a lesser wage was looked upon by persons with more humane hearts as exploitation. This phenomenon was not observed as clearly in the farms because the work places were scattered and the workers were seldom seen in large groups; nor did they have to work all year round, whereas in the factories, being compact, the exploitation, whether real or supposed, was more visible. There were surely many observers but the most prominent ones who theorised and wrote at length on the phenomenon were Karl Marx and his friend Friedrich Engels. The fruit of their efforts was the enormous thesis running into several volumes, *Das Kapital,* which is still considered the most masterly of the commentaries on capitalism. Marxism proved fecund enough to be not only an economic thesis but also a political ideology, which in the 20th century went on to rule more people than any other idea. The greater part of the world, as a result, became classless societies, the largest countries being the Soviet Union and China.

Marxism tried to achieve these classless societies by dispossessing the capitalists or the bourgeoisie of the ownership of the means of production, in effect means of making profit. The new alternative owners were not the people at large but the state run by a coterie of Marxist leaders. That in effect was state capitalism. The gigantic American corporations, with widely dispersed shareholding appeared nearer socialism than state capitalism begotten by the Marxist state. Nevertheless, this system was seen by many for many years as more just and humane; a resounding triumph of the people and the abolition of class exploitation. The countries, which had not slipped into Marxist hands, had multitudes of trade unions whose mission was to protect the interests of the workers or the proletariat.

What the followers of Marx failed to observe was the vicarious influence that Vladimir Lenin's coming to power had on the capitalist societies. The impact of the Leninist charisma was that the bourgeoisie or the owners realised that the poor man or the worker also mattered as a partner in social or state power especially in countries which functioned democratically. As a result, in these societies, the rich began giving the poor a fairer share of their economic harvest. They had to be cared for. As it happened, the communist economics proved to be wasteful and under-productive. They could not, therefore, do justice to their common folk. The capitalist societies, on the other hand, generated greater surpluses and had more to spare for their common folk. As a result, the poor man or woman in the western societies became better off than those in the economies which had undergone communist revolutions. Paradoxical no doubt; yet rulers, whether in the politburos or central committees did not take serious notice of the peculiar contradiction.

Some of those severely opposed to Communism, innovated

in Italy an ideology alternative to both the opposing theories alleged to be exploitative as well as one of conflict. They based their proposal on class collaboration and called it fascism; fascio in Italian meant 'a bundle'. Professor Alfredo Rocco, the Minister of Justice in the Mussolini cabinet, set out the gist of this new ideology in the course of a speech at Perugia in 1925. According to him, society does not exist for the individual, but the individual exists for the society; economic progress is a social interest of all. Every class of people should collaborate to maximise production. He held the interests of employers and the employees to be identical. To ensure that this was practised, there was a system of State discipline over class conflicts. Strikes and lockouts were both illegal and punishable by heavy fines and imprisonment.

Whenever possible, employers and workers in each industry, trade or profession were organised together in syndical associations. Where it was not possible to form such syndicates, the unions and the employers' associations remained but combined to form guilds to ensure coordination. If collective bargaining did not prove successful, the disputes were referred to law courts. This is how class collaboration was conceptualised by the Fascist Party. In practice, the economy was toned up by rearmament and public works. Soldiers and workers in large numbers were recruited in factories to produce goods. This would bring profits to the bourgeoisie who could then pay the proletariat well. Urban prosperity would increase demand for agricultural produce. What was left of the unemployed youth was absorbed by the armed forces. The promise for the whole nation was exports.

Another point to note was the institution of the trade union whose core objective in the capitalistic economies was to weaken the bourgeois industries. That was the way to prepare the society for a revolution. Without weakening the bourgeoisie, how would it allow a revolution? Nearer at home, Kerala and West Bengal were two interesting theatres of effective, authentic trade unionism. Over the years, in both these states, manufacturing industrial units were nearly all closed. The unions were meant to protect and promote the welfare and interests of the workers; at least prima facie. In fact, they helped the communists to come to power in the two states. In the short run, they also helped to better the lot of the workers but in the long run, the trade unions caused the industries to close and disemploy the workers. People in the states, other than Kerala and West Bengal, did not respond to the communists. Thus India was a country that witnessed the display of communism without having to pay the price of a revolution.

Europeans are generally given to analytical thinking and, in the process, they categorised the rich and the poor into classes which we have mentioned earlier. Karl Marx and his co-thinkers went on to assume that the poor cannot prosper unless they eliminate the rich by organising a revolution or otherwise. Asians, especially the Hindus, have greater faith in evolution or what the distinguished sociologist, MN Srinivas, called in the context of castes, *sanskritization*. In his view, every caste hopes, if not also aspires to go up in the Hindu hierarchy and thus become better off. At the back of the Hindu approach is the faith in deeds causing destiny, not necessarily struggle as a basis of success.

Remember, the USA, Canada, Australia did not pass through the era of feudalism in the course of which classes crystallised. As a result, perhaps such countries did not have communist movements. Wherever trade unions functioned, they were largely free of ideological baggage. All in all, it appears that there will be some rich and plenty of poor people. After the disappearance of communism, the future should lie in the cooperation or collaboration of classes.

Route to Eternity

A CLUTCH OF houses in Chhai Pokhar in Achhnera block of Agra district have turned into graveyards as some families are compelled to bury their departed in their homes due to lack of space in the burial ground. As a result, the dead here are a constant part of day-to-day life. The correspondent of a leading newspaper found women cooking next to where their children were buried while the elderly rested on cots in a backyard full of graves.

With our bourgeoning population, the man-land ratio is worsening by the day. Yet, significant areas are covered by cemeteries, *qabristans* and other graveyards. Each grave occupies at least five square yards or more considering the pathways and margins. In the case of the *qabristan*, conceptually the grave is supposed to be eternal. Long after the remains have degenerated, the land is supposed to continue to remain occupied, presumably awaiting *qayamat* or doomsday.

An appeal should, therefore, be made to everyone concerned that bodies should be cremated rather than buried, wherever a gas or an electric crematorium is available. All in all, this is a plea to the various governments to discourage Hindus from using up wood and the others from occupying land. The decision of the Madras Cemeteries Board to construct an electric crematorium at Kilpauk has testified that there was no religious obstacle between burial and cremation, at least among Christians. And Muslims are also *Ahl-e-Kitab* or belonging to a religion of the Book. The Bishops of Mylapore, Madras, have also given their consent for this break from tradition. The earlier reluctance of Christians towards cremations was their belief in resurrection. It was allowed only in emergencies like epidemics, famines or wars. Moreover, cremation was looked upon as a pagan practice; it was the practice in the pre-Christian era in Europe. In any case, the Roman Catholic Church did not permit it until 1963 when the Pope lifted the ban. Incidentally, the legendary Field Marshall Erwin Rommel of WWII Germany was cremated and not buried. Although the Jews have been conservative, Judaism does not prohibit cremation.

Cremation by burning wood is a colossal crime today against the country's disappearing forest cover and the nation's ecology. Estimates of the quantity of wood used annually for cremation across the country vary widely from 12 to 72 lakh tonnes. Regardless of the actual quantity used, it is easy to see what a waste of wood it is—wood that takes years to grow is blown up in a matter of an hour or so into smoke to dispose of a body. In the Hindu view, once the soul leaves the body, what remains is a dead mass. As India entered the tribal era, the need to get rid of the dead body must have been realised. Most of the plentiful land must have been green with a luxuriant forest cover. Burning the body was the obvious choice. The Abrahamic people chose burial because they had plenty of land but limited water and fewer trees or wood. Moreover, for them, there is a single life which finally terminates on doomsday. The body is treated with respect even after death, whereas for the Hindu the soul is all important because it is born again and again; the body without the soul is a piece of waste matter to be disposed of as soon as possible.

It is not surprising that tradition insists the body of a person who dies during the day must be cremated before sunset; that of someone who dies at night must be disposed of before sunrise. This is logical enough in a climate which is generally hot and humid. How polluted the dead body is considered to be is illustrated by what many a family in Gujarat practices. A dying person is transferred to the bare floor well before life goes out. The idea is to avoid polluting the bedding.

The ceremonial use of ghee, sandalwood etc. was introduced to help the priest to earn some money and to enable the cremating staff to make a living. The attitude towards the body is so casual that all garments are allowed to be taken away by the cremating staff before the funeral pyre is lit. True, there is a sentiment attached to *homagni* or the *havan* as an essential part of the ceremony. However, a brief *havan* in a small container can be performed without having to waste too much wood. There is, therefore, no religious or sentimental barrier to a widespread changeover to electric or gas crematoria.

Our country is awakening rapidly to the importance of ecology and environment. It is, therefore, surprising that no national leader has taken the initiative and appealed to the

Hindus to stop using wood and instead use electric or gas crematoria, wherever available. No doubt water is invaluable and we are threatened with running out of it in the coming years. But equally valuable is wood which consumes water to grow. As far as land is concerned, India has an adverse land-man ratio and it is certainly as valuable as water. Why waste it on graves? It is unfortunate that gas or electrical facilities are not being introduced with any speed in the towns and villages of India. In Europe, it is reported that 50 per cent of the final journeys are performed by cremation and only the rest by burial. Parsis have been changing over to cremation from their tradition of letting vultures devour carcasses.

At the time of Independence, on paper, India had about 25 per cent forest cover. How much was the difference between the paper records and the reality on the ground is difficult to say. It is, however, not unduly hard to believe that by now the actual forest cover would be 10 per cent or less in the country as a whole. True, poverty in some of the rural areas is so excruciating that the local people have no alternative but to live off the surrounding forest. Equally perhaps, beyond a point, the governments are not able to prevent unscrupulous traders from denuding the forests. But there can be no excuse for the policy not to be in tune with the country's ecological necessity.

Divine Right to Rule

THE MORE PEOPLE, especially politicians, criticise the Congress party for being dynastic, the more unreasonable they are. Little do they realise that there appears to be a conviction amongst the members of the leading family that they have a divine right to rule India. It began in 1946 when the party needed to elect a new president. Maulana Abul Kalam Azad had been the head for six years in a row, largely due to the Quit India movement and most of the leaders being in jail. Moreover, by 1946, Independence was in the air with the Labour Party in power in Britain. As per the standard practice, the party secretariat asked the Pradesh Congress Committees (PCC) for their preference of the candidate. The majority wanted Patel but Gandhi intervened asking him to step aside and let Jawaharlal be the president. Patel obeyed and Gandhi asked the Working Committee to select Nehru.

The 1946 presidency was important because its incumbent would head any central government that was formed thereafter. So did Nehru; first as vice-president of the Interim Government under the Viceroy as resident. On 15 August 1947, Jawaharlal Nehru was automatically chosen the prime minister. He was specially selected and anointed by the Father of the Nation as Gandhi was called—a unique honour and a rare gesture. It would give anyone the message that he was very special, especially if one recollects that in his lifetime Gandhi was beginning to be considered by some as the tenth avatar of Vishnu.

Few doubted that Nehru wanted his daughter Indira to succeed him. K Kamaraj, the President of the Congress Party possibly knew of Nehru's wish. But 1964 was the time when political life was restrained by decorum and leaders did not behave as uninhibitedly as they do now. Kamaraj did not allow an open election by the parliamentary party but held a secret survey of the Lok Sabha members as to who was their choice. According to the survey, the majority favoured Lal Bahadur Shastri in preference to Morarji Desai. The difference between the secret survey and an open election was doubt in place of transparency. People in Gujarat and elsewhere also suspected that perhaps Kamaraj had chosen a weak and relatively colourless candidate. When the 1967 general elections came he could perhaps be persuaded to step aside in favour of Indira Gandhi who presumably would be a more attractive leader electorally. Thus no one would point a finger at Nehru for having nominated his daughter as his successor. A gap of sixteen months between the father's demise and the daughter's succession respected decorum which now one would not have. This inhibition was abandoned when Indira Gandhi was assassinated in October 1984. A dozen or more bullets were pumped into her body by her bodyguards.

According to informal reports of the AIIMS hospital, she was brought in dead. By 11 am, the BBC radio had reported her death. But the Akashvani (Indian radio) reported the shooting much later although Rajiv Gandhi had returned in early afternoon from Kalaikunda military airport; he happened to be on a visit to West Bengal. But Rashtrapati Giani Zail Singh was away in West Asia and by the time he could return it was a little before 6 pm at which time Rajiv was sworn in as prime minister. This was constitutionally an irregular way of electing a PM. When Nehru died, Gulzarilal Nanda, the senior most in the cabinet was sworn in as an interim incumbent promptly until the new candidate was duly elected by the Lok Sabha parliamentary party, as indeed Shastri was. Shastri died at Tashkent and Indira Gandhi was duly elected by the parliamentary party.

It was only then that Nanda, who had again been the interim PM, stepped aside. The same procedure should have been followed after Indira's demise. The two senior cabinet ministers were Narasimha Rao and Pranab Mukherjee; either could have been interim PM until the formal election by the parliamentary party, in this case of Rajiv Gandhi. Earlier his brother Sanjay Gandhi was reputed to behave as Indira's crown prince of the old eras. He held no elected or appointed position in 1974 and was, therefore, an extra-constitutional entity. Yet he exercised autocratic powers at least in Delhi.

When the Allahabad High Court unseated Indira Gandhi from the Lok Sabha in early June 1975, she declared an internal emergency and went on to abolish the rights of citizens given by Articles 15 and 16 of the Constitution. Or else, how could the divine right to rule be perpetuated? In contrast, when Atal Bihari

Vajpayee government fell by one vote in 1999, he promptly resigned and sought re-election. That one vote was ethically questionable because Giridhar Gomango, a Lok Sabha member, had become chief minister of Orissa and was governing the state. Yet he sneaked into the Lok Sabha and voted.

When the Emergency came, Sanjay Gandhi expressed noble sentiments for the country. He appealed to the people to talk less and work more; he wanted to clean up and smarten the cities as well as control the exploding population. He was told that Muslims particularly have more children than others. He, however, did not know that the Hadith, also an Islamic scripture, prohibits birth control. It is alleged that Sanjay nominated Rukhsana Sultana (Hindu name Meenu Bimbet), a fashionable socialite of Delhi, to persuade the Muslims of Shahjehanabad to limit their families as well as to transfer to allotted plots in trans-Yamuna and vacate their illegal quarters near the Turkman Gate and surroundings. Sultana made Dujana House her headquarters for *nasbandi* operations on both men and women. Inevitably, mayhem followed with tear gas, firing and resultant deaths on quite a large scale.

Since Nehru was anointed by Gandhi in 1946, a great deal of democratic water has flowed under the bridge. Several commoners have been prime ministers since and yet, the Nehru family has not modified its old royal ways. The party presidentship is bouncing like a shuttlecock between Sonia Gandhi and her son today.

Cricket Calls for Reforms

CRICKET IN INDIA is not merely a sport, but also a career to earn money and become rich. It is a generator of wealth and a significant contributor to the Gross Domestic Product (GDP) of the national economy. Moreover, it is a platform to arouse and enjoy patriotism. Indians, especially Hindus, have achieved few military victories against foreign countries. Winning against Pakistan, whether in Kashmir, Bangladesh or Kargil is akin to winning in what is basically a civil war. The last military victory against an actual foreigner was achieved by Chandragupta Maurya. This was in 303 BC when he defeated and expelled Seleucus I, successor of Alexander the Great in Bactria.

Cricket began as a game for gentlemen at leisure to pass time. This was in the south of England. In due course, interest in the game spread to the British colonies of Australia and New

Zealand and later to India thanks to the East India Company. The sport got going in the 19th century. Strangely, the Americas did not take to cricket, although North America had been a British colony; the USA and Canada preferred baseball. Cricketers in the early days mostly came from the aristocracy and were called 'gentlemen'. But not always could the gentlemen find 22 willing players; they found volunteers from among the gardeners and other staff members. Those not from the upper echelons were called 'players' as distinct from the aristocracy, who insistently remained 'gentlemen'. The players were given a separate pavilion gate to use and they wrote their first names while the gentlemen distinguished themselves by using their initials like PFR and not Peter. Players were not made captains of their teams until Len Hutton was picked by England in the year 1952. India also copied the tradition by selecting princes like the Maharaja of Vizianagaram or Patiala or the Nawab of Pataudi (his father Iftikhar Ali and not Tiger Pataudi whom we are familiar with).

There was also a time when the Thomas Cup in badminton used to be an event of national interest. The Indian team was for years a contender for the world championship. TN Seth and Suresh Goel, followed by the outstanding Nandu Natekar as well as Prakash Padukone, all held national attention in the realm of the shuttlecock. Domestic cricket tournaments have not aroused much crowd interest. In a Ranji or Duleep Trophy, or the Irani Cup match there is hardly any audience. Yet in the 1930s, the games of the Quadrangular tournament provided thrills and were lapped up by crowds. The most popular matches were those between Hindus and Muslims, the prototype of India-Pakistan contests. Parsis and Europeans evoked limited response.

There was a phase when Ramanathan Krishnan followed by the Amritraj brothers made national news in tennis. Football also had its spell of mass following in West Bengal and the south. The IFA Shield was quite an annual event. Internationally, India was represented in the 1948 London Olympics but, unfortunately, we lost to France in the first round. For decades now, we have not qualified for the Olympics. Understandably, the lack of international success took its toll on the sport's popularity at home.

Earlier, wrestling too had its phase of glory with names like Gama, Imam Bux and Goonga, who have still not been forgotten. Vishwanathan Anand has brought the intellectual game of chess to the forefront and has made India a world champion in it. There are several grandmasters and it is hoped that this game, which is believed to have been invented in India, will flourish more and more.

Unlike football or hockey, a cricket captain can be as important as three or four players. Think of the difference that Clive Lloyd made to West Indies cricket. The captain should be the first player to be chosen, not only for his ability to bat or bowl but for his capability for captaincy. The late Ashok Mankad is a name that comes to mind as an example of this contention. The normal practice is to select the best available combination of eleven players. Thereafter, the most suitable among the eleven, usually a batsman, must be chosen as the skipper. Mahendra Singh Dhoni was selected as a wicketkeeper and blossomed into an excellent captain.

Given the planning, foresight and innovativeness, there is no reason why India should not dominate world cricket indefinitely. It not only has the best batting side but also has a tradition of innovation. The most original contribution made by an Indian to cricket was by Maharaja Jam Sahib of Navanagar. Until his advent, deliberate scoring strokes were confined to the front of the wicket. It was Ranji who innovated the leg glance, pull and sweep. To quote from Alan Ross's book, *Ranji* (London, 1983), "He can place to leg within a foot of where he wishes almost any ball that pitches between wicket and wicket. He has a slight prejudice against forward play for forcing strokes".

On the off-side, the cut, whether lemon, late or plain, came into common use after Ranji's time. To quote again from Alan Ross, "The Indian has the eye of the hawk and wrists like Toledo steel, and the finest of the batsman's art is his timing of the ball. He has a late cut which the envious gods are still practicing in the Elysian Fields".

The wicketkeeper cannot bowl but the remaining ten players can hypothetically bat, bowl, as well as field. In other words, if every team member did everything well, there would be 32 roles performed. The day would come before long when this should happen. And the day may not be far when enterprising teams would go beyond the 32 roles, when some bowlers would be able to bowl with both arms. If a boy has the aptitude for bowling, why not coach him to use his left as well as his right arm? There are players who bat and bowl with different arms like Sourav Ganguly or Vinoo Mankad and John Goddard, the West Indian captain of yesteryears. Why cannot such players bowl with both the arms? Or even bat with both hands; the batsman is then ready to deal effectively with different bowlers. Such could be the all-rounders of the future. And the training of 10 or 12-year-old youngsters should begin now.

In a Test match, the burden of attack is on the bowler whereas in a one-day game the onus is on the batsman. Why not ask the faster bowlers not to worry about speed but to concentrate on accuracy? Years ago, Bapu Nadkarni used to bowl immaculately, so much so that it was said he could land his ball on the same spot four or five times in an over. In one test match innings his bowling analysis was 30 overs, 27 maidens, 7 runs and 0 wickets His length was perfect but there was no guile in his bowling. In the one-day game, Nadkarni would be an invaluable asset. The batsmen facing him would get so impatient that they would make mistakes.

The Sino-Indian Tango

THE SINO-INDIAN equation was designed by architect VK Krishna Menon soon after Mao Zedong captured power in Peking (now Beijing) in 1949. Prime Minister Jawaharlal Nehru bought it wholesale and quite uncritically. Menon was at heart a communist and in his head a pseudo-Congressman. In those early days, most reds believed that no communist could betray another. China should therefore be befriended as Nehru's efforts were on to cultivate Stalin's Soviet Union. His own sister Vijayalakshmi Pandit was the first envoy to Moscow rather than a professional diplomat. Similarly, everything was to be done to please China.

Deputy Prime Minister Sardar Patel, on the other hand, wrote in a letter to Nehru dated 7 November 1950, that the last action of the Chinese was little short of perfidy. 'The tragedy of it is that the Tibetans put faith in us. The communist mentality is whoever is not with them is against them'. Patel went on to say, 'The situation that faces us is that Tibet will soon disappear'. Thirty-eight days later the Sardar died and with him his wisdom was also cremated. Nehru could then be freely guided by his friend Menon. Between the two they looked upon China as an elder brother and did what it wished India to do. Meanwhile, Peking built a road through Aksai Chin linking Tibet with its western province of Sinkiang. In 1962, India was humiliated and deprived of 30,000 square Km of our territory.

The Indian people, till this day, have not recovered from the trauma of 1962 and hope that someday we will get back the territory. There was no harm in hoping but we could not even think independently of how to deal with China. It was only after the advent of Prime Minister Modi that a clear and welcome change became visible. Nevertheless, our economy did remain dependent on Chinese imports at the cost of a huge trade deficit every year. We remained apparently duty bound to be friendly rather than adversarial even after the Doklam skirmish. Only the Galwan valley clash has openly made us adversaries. The Modi government's attention to military preparedness has to be acknowledged. Incidentally, Nehru had once written that since we believe in peace, we do not need an army; our police was sufficient.

Now that we have recognised the stark reality, half the problem stands solved as savant Jiddu Krishnamurti might have said. Now we can focus and concentrate on the other half. We have to try and reduce imports from China even if similar material or goods cost more elsewhere. In most cases, even if the manufacturer incurs ten per cent expenditure he/she can manage to absorb it. Most imports are only a percentage of the product. Even otherwise cutting costs intelligently is part of the art of an industrial manager. The World Trade Organization (WTO) is getting defunct and we should not be inhibited by its excessive insistence on free exports and imports.

Normally, it is desirable for all countries to have allies. India has been inhibited by a Nehruvian myth of non-alignment. Even in his time, India was a subordinate or a dependent ally of the Soviet Union. After the 1965 war with Pakistan, the post-war peace talks took place in Tashkent under the auspices of the Soviet Prime Minster Kosygin. In the 1971 war, the Soviets underwrote our safety against the USA which was sympathetic to Pakistan.

An alliance is not a sacramental marriage which is permanent until death parts the spouses. Alliances are for mutual interest for specific purposes. It is not an ideological identification as Krishna Menon appeared to have convinced Nehru. Communism introduced the ideological obsession. Until then nations functioned freely; some might have been influenced by religion, whether Christianity or Islam. Even that is all getting over now. United Arab Republic and Bahrain have established diplomatic relations recently. India can have an alliance with any number of countries against China and that too for specific functions. Say, an Indo-French treaty may be for temporary supply of war planes in the event of war. In return, we can commit to acquire aircraft from France. Similarly, the USA can underwrite nuclear help with its own missiles and pilots in the event of need. In return, Americans can outsource manufacture of fighter planes like F-16 to India.

With Australia, too, a treaty could be entered into, with India being allowed to have a base in the northern part of the country, in return for which India would be ready to lend its army.

When it comes to Japan, a quasi-alliance is already in place with Tokyo. If upgraded to a full-fledged one, India and Japan will benefit mutually. India's vast army can meet Japan's need for ground troops; the Indian army's combat experience of decades will be invaluable. In return, India can benefit from Japan's technology.

Such alliances would make India's ability to fight much greater. It would place the country in a position to settle all outstanding differences. From India's point of view, the present is an appropriate time to settle differences, for China has gathered several adversarial relationships, from the USA in the West to Japan in the East. There are pressures against the yellow giant from its export markets. We do not know if the president of China has domestic pressures against him, but we can be certain that his being declared president for life in this 21st century would not be welcome. For one, such an election would be looked upon as antediluvian. For another, what about the ambitious of many other leaders? There are times when there arise opportunities for progressive moves. This is when a country cannot afford to sit back. India has arrived at such a point of time. A year earlier, circumstances were different.

Kamala Harris's Campaign

THERE IS NO doubt that Kamala Harris, the Democratic Vice-President and Joe Biden's mate, has campaigned with energy and extraordinary enthusiasm. Her emphasis on the USA being divided between blacks and whites, apart from causing a flutter in the roost, is not correct. The country can be more accurately described as multi-coloured with people of different hues. When Biden invited her to be his running mate, she insistently declared herself to be a black. During her campaign, Harris also talked of *dosa* and filter coffee, reflective of her association also with Chennai.

In Indian election campaigns, the contestants do not introduce themselves. The reasoning is that they are supposed to be leaders and, therefore, well known. They do not carry their visiting cards. Whether this practice applies to the USA or not, I do not know. Ms Harris's familiarity with American history is impressive, but it might have been better if she did not raise from the platform the issue of "one country, two systems". That must be so, but for a candidate it may not be desirable; emphasising the fact carries the peril of a likely polarisation of the electorate along the lines of black versus white.

For a white candidate, the remark could pass, but for an Indian/black lady to declare her deep sympathy for blacks would mark her as a clear proponent of identity. The opposition could retaliate by alleging that Kamala Harris has come out to represent the blacks of America. Biden could look after white interests while the others should fend for themselves. Carrying the logic further, a Republican Party supporter could raise the question: what happens if Mr Biden happens to resign midway? Who would be President for 85 per cent of America? Mind you, these comments are based on Indian experience. To give an example, Babu Jagjivan Ram in his 34-year long career (1946-1979) in the Indian Cabinet, never once talked about his caste, or that he was a Dalit. His reasoning was that to become prime minister, he would have to have the support of all the various castes. The Dalits across India would not exceed 15 per cent. How far would that carry me? He would ask in private. Unfortunately, he did not become prime minister, but retired from politics as deputy prime minister of India in 1979.

Anybody who has a sensitive conscience would sympathise with the suffering the blacks have undergone for centuries. How they were captured from their homes and dragged out and sold to white traders who regularly visited West Africa. They were then packed into ships in abnormally large numbers as if they were goods and not living beings. There were no toilets for them in these ships because they occupied the holds and not the cabins. Before they reached the coasts of the New World, up to 30 per cent of the black passengers would have died; the dead bodies were flung into the ocean. There was no question of a coffin or any ceremony.

Fortunately, William Wilberforce, an active member of Britain's House of Commons, spent most of his political career trying to abolish this barbaric trade in slaves. More fortunately, William Pitt the Younger was his friend. Pitt remained prime minister for twenty-two years and supported Wilberforce in his efforts for the abolition of the slave trade. Once England stopped trading in slaves, other countries too slowed down and stopped. Once the slaves were sold, the barbaric treatment suffered during the ship voyages no doubt stopped but the tale of long oppression began.

A glimpse of the oppression of slavery is eloquently depicted in the famous novel *Uncle Tom's Cabin* by Harriet Beecher Stowe. However well some masters and their families treated their slaves, they could not appreciate how miserable human life was as a slave, completely devoid of aspirations. Another facet of slavery from the work point of view is interesting. The Yankees or North Americans who ran industries came to the conclusion that the productivity of an average slave was less than that of a paid worker. In other words, it was better to employ and pay a wage than forcibly extract work out of a slave. This was one of the reasons why the Yankees supported abolition of slavery and even the Civil War. The Confederate southerners were obsessed with large labour forces to run their plantations, whether of cotton or any other produce. No doubt, in the America of those early decades, so much manpower, other than the slaves, was not available.

For Ms Harris, it may be useful to praise President Barack

Hussein Obama. To push the black point of view and talk about Floyd George and other murders would be music to the ears of black people. But such examples are likely to give offence to many a white voter. He or she would feel that the candidate is trying to tease their conscience. This is the same logic that influenced Babu Jagjivan Ram. In any case, it has been said by the wise that a victim is not his own best advocate. The other factor which Ms Harris would be unaware of is that a brown person, whether Indian or any other, can be as prejudiced against blacks as some whites are. If she were to live in India for a little while, she would discover this for herself.

An interesting question would be—what might have been the calculation that motivated Joe Biden to select Kamala Harris as his running mate? The women's vote is probably the largest segment in an American election. But then, why has there been only one Presidential candidate so far? Hillary Clinton was expected to do well, but Donald Trump came from behind and overtook her at the last moment. Governor Sarah Palin of Alaska, although articulate and active, could not help Senator John McCain perform better, if not also win; McCain eventually lost to Obama. For the success of the Biden team, a disproportionate responsibility rests on Kamala Harris's shoulders. For one, he is old; for another, he has not shone with success in any presidential contest.

The fact that women have not been able to do better in American politics ought to be a subject of questioning and research by the Kamala Harris electoral team. The so-called South Asian subcontinent has done far better in this context. Indira Gandhi was prime minister; so was Benazir Bhutto, Prime Minister of Pakistan. Bangladesh has produced two women prime ministers—Sheikh Hasina Wazed and Begum

Khaleda Zia. Sri Lanka has thrown up Sirimavo Bandarnaike and later her daughter Chandrika Kumaratunga.

Could this be attributed to the fact that the Hindu civilization is almost unique in traditionally worshipping female deities? Eastern India is dominated by goddesses, beginning with Durga, Kali, Lakshmi, Saraswati and many others. This is not a new phenomenon. In Vedic times, women were virtually equals of men, educationally and socially. So much so, that even Islam in this region has been influenced by this Hindu tradition. Not merely Pakistan and Bangladesh, but even Indonesia and possibly Burma have been similarly influenced. Megawati Sukarnoputri has been Indonesia's President while Aung San Suu Kyi is the State Counsellor (a position equivalent to prime minister) of Myanmar (Burma). Has religion been the inspiration in Asia? Otherwise, why should an advanced country like the United States of America be so much behind in this context of gender justice?

Much Ado About Immigrants

MUSLIMS IN THE Indian subcontinent have enjoyed a many-splendoured life over the last millennia. Muslims began coming first to Malabar in Kerala, then to Sind and then through the Hindu Kush Pass. They began coming as Arab traders, as short-term conquerors, as converters of *kafirs* to Islam whether with the help of Sufis or otherwise, as robbers as did Mahmud of Ghazni and later as conquerors/rulers to stay as did Muhammad Ghori.

Christians did not begin by coming in any numbers but by getting converted when St Thomas arrived in Kerala in 58AD from West Asia. There was no fighting or loot. In course of time many more Christians came to India as missionaries, whether to tend to the sick or teach the children. The primary thrust of the followers of Christ was service and then conversion of faith.

After 1600 AD, there was an entirely novel development and that was the East India Company using its Crown Charter to trade in India. While expanding its trade, it gradually captured India and while doing so helped many parts of India to be relieved of their Muslim rulers who were unwelcome, like Nawab Siraj-ud-Daulah of Bengal and Tipu Sultan of Mysore. To go back into history, the Qutbuddin Aibak sultanate began in 1206 and the Mughal in 1858. Despite a long and titanic Hindu struggle against Islamic rulers, the process was hastened with Robert Clive of East India Company who defeated the Nawab of Bengal at the Battle of Plassey in 1757. Lord Wellesley defeated and killed Tipu Sultan in 1799. Finally, Lord Dalhousie dismissed Nawab Wajid Ali Shah of Awadh. Then the Sepoy Mutiny of 1857-58 took place.

The mutiny resulted in 90 years of the rule of the British Crown and then finally came independence. Would India have got freedom so systematically from any of the nawabs? Would the country have become one? Would any of its parts have become modern? The benefits of British rule are well-known. Should not the British government be treated as Christian? There have been no Hindu-Christian riots though some British officers had been killed by young Hindu extremists. These facts and arguments are put forward in order to ensure peace and harmony. In the words of Dr Ambedkar, there was a civil war between the Hindus and Muslims between the years 1920 and 1940. That clash was part of the movement that ended in Partition. There is no scope for another division; in which case where would the current polarisation lead to? There are no longer any British officers; only Indians in charge of the Indian police, paramilitary forces and armed forces. The history of India or Hindu-Muslim relations would be of no help. If anything they would provide provocation, if not also instigation. Only sense and wisdom can help.

Some non-Muslims are seen as being eager to help the Muslim agitators, but they have a limited stake. They would, therefore, take cover at the sight of the first eruption of a fire. Only the Muslims would be out in the open. It is not that the Christians like everything that is happening; an instance is the close watch being kept over foreign donations coming to help missionary work. But Christian leaders keep restraint and seldom protest publicly. Years ago when some people had damaged a few churches, they protested in a civil manner but did not resort to litigation. They recalled that in their time Christians too had demolished a few temples in the South.

Imams and maulanas, by contrast, see what their communities suffer but conveniently forget their perpetration on the Hindus. Some of them probably feel that in those times they were the rulers. They indeed were, but when the Hindus are in a majority, could they not relent at Ayodhya? Many Hindus would tend to overlook the obstinacy of the All India Personal Law Board but not all Hindus. Many a Hindu would appreciate and remember the gesture of the Shia Board in letting go its claim, if any. But not all Hindus might be so magnanimous; they would prefer to recall that Qaid-e-Azam Jinnah was the architect of Pakistan. These details are unimportant but they are strong and dry enough to be ready gunpowder for a potential civil war. No sensible Indian should welcome such a horror, especially because in internecine fighting, it is the poor and the innocent who are more the victims. The mischief-makers and the really guilty get away scot-free.

In the heat of excitement, unintended things are said and done. On the evening of 20 February 2020, one legislator Waris

Pathan said that "15 crore Muslims would be too many for 100 crore Hindus". Those who listened to him interpreted his threat as one of a riot. In an hour or two, he had to calm down and regret his statement. Nevertheless, he had done the damage. There are other politicians who are spitting fire, though not yet beyond the line of parliamentary propriety. One can only hope that restraint will prevail before it is too late.

Not only in India, but other subcontinental equations have changed since the days of Partition. Pakistan is no longer one country. Islam has failed to hold the country together. Bangladesh is as Bengali as it is Muslim. The remaining Pakistan has fallen out with a number of its old allies and finds itself in an unhappy economic situation. Looking back, evidently the earlier years of Islamabad were its halcyon days.

An article published in the *Pioneer* in 2005 stated that World War IV had commenced; many a country of the world was at war with Muslims. Even domestically, things are not the same as before. Could anyone have expected ten years ago that a large number of Muslim women would unilaterally approach the Supreme Court for prohibiting instant *triple talaq*? This judgment was followed up by Parliament with a virtually unanimous legislation. These steps have been followed by some more women petitioning for a common civil code. Whether these changes are sustained and go on to become a reality is another matter. What is obvious is that the Muslim men and women are no longer as united as before.

The lesson of history is that generally right wins over wrong, the moral over the immoral. Rama triumphed over Ravana; the Pandavas prevailed over the Kauravas. During World War II, the Allied side appeared to be losing. It was touch and go till the tide turned and eventually democracy and the free way of life won and the totalitarian dictatorship was defeated. The result of the Cold War was the same; freedom and democracy won while the totalitarian ideology and system suffered a resounding defeat. Why all this risk and trouble for the illegal migrants, whether from Bangladesh or Pakistan? Neither CAA, NRC nor NPR threaten the Indian Muslims.

New Dawn for the Military

WOMEN SOLDIERS WOULD be a serious problem if and when they happen to be taken prisoner. Here we propose to discuss commanding officers who are seldom in the first line of infantry fighting or artillery duels, nor are cavalry officers acutely vulnerable. This question of POWs has possibly confused the whole issue of command qualities. The question of strength and stamina has fortunately been resolved as infantry weapons became light and more efficient. There is no comparison between the .303 and today's assault rifle. The writer, too, found the former heavy to lift and carry for long.

The issue of women as jawans or officers was unfairly influenced by tradition and mindset. Until firearms came into existence, the prospects for women were hopeless as the sword or the lance were heavy and needed strong arms. Women were also weaker due to the quality of diet and more so due to the number of childbirths. Mumtaz Mahal, queen of Shah Jahan, possibly the wealthiest man in the world of his time, bore fourteen children of whom only seven survived. Imagine the waste of female stamina and strength! How could women be soldiers? She who cannot be a soldier, cannot be an officer and, in turn, a commander. To add to this was the mindset and all the biases against women except as householders and mothers.

The invention of the musket in the 16th century sprouted the first ray of hope for the woman as a soldier. The gender of the individual pressing the trigger made no difference to the target. The early models, however, were very heavy, and were often operated by two soldiers resting the weapon on a portable table. This innovation by itself limited the chances for the woman; nevertheless, it was a beginning, an opening which no one could then visualise. After that, the better and lighter the weapon, the lesser the muscle or stamina required. The less the childbearing, the stronger the woman remained. We have travelled so far through four to five centuries.

This is a new dawn for the military. The armed forces have many more potential candidates to choose from now. And the women can make equally good fighters—whether on land, air or sea. In fact, in defensive engagements, they could well be superior to men. For instance, a tigress or any female animal protects her young quite ferociously. When a woman defends her homeland, the writer believes she would be equally committed, if not more than the men. A brave man would defend his country with equal zeal but when he finds his situation hopeless, he may be likely to retreat or even surrender. A woman is less likely to give up. An order like 'Victory or death' is less difficult for a woman to obey than for a man. The apparently braver the commander, the more courageous would be the battalion.

The recent doubt which the Supreme Court had to clear about whether women officers would make equally effective commanders is unusual. The male ego, fattened since the beginning of time, could find it difficult to obey a woman in public. In private, it is different. Shorn of such mindsets the issue is one of leadership. In the 1960s who could have believed that Indira Gandhi would have made a leader superior to say, Morarji Desai? The question is one of leadership and not of statesmanship or prime ministership. Gandhi retained the leadership of the Congress Party until her death. True, she had the advantage of being Jawaharlal Nehru's daughter which gave her an enviable start. After that, she had to rely on her own wit and resources in order to survive and succeed.

The problem hitherto has been that women did not get the exposure and opportunity to be able to perform on the right platform and at the right level, at least in most fields. Kanshi Ram gave a start to Mayawati and she came up to be the chief minister of UP. Mamata Banerjee has risen exclusively on her own initiative; she has demonstrated eloquently what are the qualities needed to make nine crore people of West Bengal follow her.

For some time, maybe some years, the women commanders would have to develop superior qualities such as military knowledge, bold initiative and quick decision-making. Leaders must be superior to their followers. Once that is demonstrated, there should be no difficulty.

The Elphinstone college in Mumbai had no grounds and hence the PT was held at the neighbouring Oval maidan. The entire class of 110 students would together move to this ground.

There were less than 25 boys and the rest were girls. The latter were given light exercises which could be done while wearing sarees, which were what most girls wore at that time. The boys, however, had to sprint, do sit-ups, push-ups et al. The writer was not strong and could do no more than 15 to 17 push-ups. At the Oval, however, in the presence of the girls, he could go up to 50 of them. The only explanation was the gender pride. How could he let his pride down? If this gender pride could percolate to the armed forces, we could expect extraordinary performance from our sailors, soldiers and airmen.

When we move from the commander to the level of a senior general, the situation could change. The progress from tactics to strategy is a big leap. The former is adequate for a skirmish or a limited battle. Anything bigger would call for greater military imagination—to be able to visualise what is neither visible nor obvious. A strategy must ensure that the war plan is not upset even if the future brings forth enemy action that is surprisingly different. World War II German Field Marshal, Erwin Rommel, is probably the most famous general. When compared with Field Marshal Erich von Manstein, Rommel is considered an exceptional tactician; whereas Manstein, by his defence in depth strategy, delayed the Russian army from reaching Germany by a whole year. The Manstein brilliance lay in retreating faster than the Russians could move, then waiting on the sidelines until the Reds had arrived only to be surrounded and taken prisoners in thousands.

France has six borders beginning with the North Sea in the west, then Belgium, then the German border which was defended by a chain of fortresses called the Maginot line. The Ardennes forest was considered impassable. Berlin was in search of a point of the surprise attack. Manstein suggested the presumably impassable Ardennes forest. France had left it undefended; his idea was accepted. It took only forty days to make France surrender. That was a gem of a strategy.